The Wrong Emphasis

Other Books by John Elling Tufte

Crazy-Proofing High School Sports

The Wrong Emphasis

Kids Learn What Adults Teach

John Elling Tufte

ROWMAN & LITTLEFIELD
Lanham • Boulder • New York • London

Published by Rowman & Littlefield
A wholly owned subsidiary of The Rowman & Littlefield Publishing Group, Inc.
4501 Forbes Boulevard, Suite 200, Lanham, Maryland 20706
www.rowman.com

16 Carlisle Street, London W1D 3BT, United Kingdom

Copyright © 2014 by John Elling Tufte

All rights reserved. No part of this book may be reproduced in any form or by any electronic or mechanical means, including information storage and retrieval systems, without written permission from the publisher, except by a reviewer who may quote passages in a review.

British Library Cataloguing in Publication Information Available

Library of Congress Cataloging-in-Publication Data available

ISBN 978-1-4758-0338-9 (cloth : alk. paper)
ISBN 978-1-4758-0339-6 (pbk. : alk. paper)
ISBN 978-1-4758-0340-2 (electronic)

∞ ™ The paper used in this publication meets the minimum requirements of American National Standard for Information Sciences Permanence of Paper for Printed Library Materials, ANSI/NISO Z39.48-1992.

Printed in the United States of America

Contents

Preface   vii
Introduction   xi

Part One: Where We Are
1. The Ugly Truth   3
2. Cultural Responsibility   11
3. Political Rhetoric   19

Part Two: Blaming the Scale
4. Andrew, 1990s   29
5. Teachers or Secretaries?   37
6. The Unwritten Curriculum   43

Part Three: Great Habits of the Unwritten Curriculum
7. Age-Appropriate Thinking Skills   53
8. Age-Appropriate People and Communication Skills   61
9. Timeliness and Attendance   69
10. Work Ethic and Dedication   77
11. Respect, Decency, and Humility   85
12. Responsibility and Teamwork   95
13. Perspective   103

Part Four: Conclusion
14. Autonomy   113

Index   121
About the Author   129

Preface

Public education in the United States continues to be one of our nation's strongest attributes. The successes we accomplish in K–12 schools are the backbone for the successes we accomplish as a country, and no other society on earth can claim to have developed a more inclusive method of educating its young people.

Nearly every child in America can receive a free public education, and we all benefit because of it. The American public school system, however, is at a crossroads—and it has been sitting at this intersection for decades.

No one close to public schools can reasonably deny that problems exist with the education of our nation's youth. In fact, most leaders in the K–12 arena acknowledge the reality that millions of our children and young adults are sadly deficient in both what they know and what they are capable of doing.

This is difficult to comprehend because, as has been the case for generations, the United States is also responsible for some of the brightest and most capable young people on the planet. Millions of children and adolescents in this country are experiencing successes their grandparents could not have imagined, they are balancing countless activities and the associated responsibilities, and our most impressive young people are well poised to transition from their public schools to colleges, universities, and the workforce in the years to come.

So what is the issue? How are our public schools stalled at the intersection? A few troubling realities coincide with the young people "thriving" in our school systems. First, we have a growing number of children and adolescents who, upon graduating from high school, are nowhere near skilled enough for colleges, universities, or the well-paying workforce.

Second, and equally as troubling, we have a population of intelligent, talented, able-bodied young people who either have no interest in striving for success, no clue what it means to work toward their aspirations, or no idea what genuine accomplishment feels like—and these are often the same children we describe as "thriving."

Indeed, there are impressive youths in our country. They are poised with their talents to work diligently and become leaders. Throughout our nation's history, however, these highly talented and driven children and young adults have clearly been the exception, not the rule (it makes sense that there are fewer above average than average).

Furthermore, despite our wishes, an immensely uncomfortable situation exists: the number of adequately prepared, primed-for-success young adults is becoming dwarfed by the masses of their aimless, unambitious, unimpressive, and somehow incredibly comfortable peers.

If the answer to these problems were simple, this book could end now. Unfortunately, the conundrum within our current world of public education reaches far beyond the question of whether or not enough of our students are performing well enough in and out of school, for we know they are not. Rather, we are struggling with what we should be doing about it. This is the puzzle we educators cannot seem to solve.

Those outside of our classrooms, however, have been all too willing with attempts to solve this problem for us. Their solutions for our "failing" schools and students? High-voltage curriculum, assessment, and accountability. The concept of assessment and accountability is often simple; the experts (including politicians and other officials far removed from our classrooms) decide what should be known or levels of proficiency, they assess these proficiencies, and those falling short are held accountable.

In many ways, admittedly, a reasonable emphasis on curriculum (Core Standards, for example), assessment, and accountability can assist educators in our country. After all, it is unlikely we can effectively teach our young people if we do not know what it is we want them to know or how we will determine their level of comprehension.

Further, it only makes sense that we educators own a great portion of the responsibility associated with student learning. Teaching America's children with neither a plan nor accountability is irresponsible; this cannot be debated.

Education, however, is not akin to effectively managing a grocery store; our work is endlessly more complicated and more important. Weeding out poorly performing students, families, and schools is not an option in the United States, for even the most insensitive among us must admit that maintaining a huge portion of uneducated, unaccomplished citizens is a burden on all of us—and that is to say nothing about the wrongs done and the misery allotted to those truly struggling to succeed within our schools. Yet somehow our angst to attain great test scores leads to the fear of school districts losing funding as a result of poor outcomes.

Sure, none of us wants to claim our educational practices are designed to "weed out" certain schools, teachers, students, and their respective families. The ideology behind school standards, assessment, and accountability is that poorly performing schools will be thrown into the education crucible, and, as though the poor performance is the result of a simple oversight among the teachers and administrators within these substandard schools, they will become adequately motivated to change their substandard ways.

As of now, there appears to be only one problem with this philosophy: it does not work. How is this possible? It has happened because our incessant need to test and prove ourselves competent has made us educators focus on our "game days" to the point that we have neglected our obligation to practice. Although great teachers and administrators across the nation consistently lament the lack of time working with their students in the place of the ever-increasing test dates, our game-day focus has proven itself to be priority number one in most public school districts.

Some schools, of course, have been the steady beacon of academic excellence during our assessment craze—or at least we are asked to believe that. When adequate yearly progress (AYP) has been accomplished, and the educators within a community allow themselves a collective exhale, it is easy to forget that these kids likely find reading tests easy because their parents were reading to them since birth. Of course, the curriculum, assessment, and accountability experts prefer to avoid some of the realities associated with test scores and parent involvement.

Most of our school districts, however, struggle to claim resounding success with AYP. We have even invented creative ways either to prolong the misery of accountability or to excuse ourselves from the process altogether—at least until the next wave of tests. Regardless, the school districts under the most pressure to improve (and the students who need the most immediate attention) have not improved using the measure-monger methodology.

Sadly, leaders in these struggling school districts have been forced to spend their time balanced between testing and finding accountability loopholes. Teaching? Learning? Thinking? We cannot measure these; we simply assume they are happening.

Even our best students have suffered from this cascade of measurements. At the very least, we have been telling ourselves that our "best and brightest" will excel on both our test days and in the years following high school graduation—right? Although there are certainly successful young people in higher education, most K–12 leaders are horribly misled about the effectiveness of the education their school districts have been emphasizing.

American colleges and universities are jam-packed with freshman boasting a 3.8 (or better) high school grade point average and a 25 ACT score, and many of these kids have never really been asked to write, discuss, struggle with, or solve anything that could not fit into a rubric.

These youths sang in their high school choir, they played two or three sports, they were on the student council, and they have traveled to some really cool destinations with their church youth group. They are great kids, and they have the trophies to prove it. Shockingly few of them, however, have actually been pushed to do anything truly difficult in school.

Droves of students like these attend college for at least some time, and many are back home before Thanksgiving. Why? (Here is where our measure-mongers need to be held down to learn something.) To begin, a high school GPA has become almost irrelevant. Countless 4.0 students, for example, are attending universities with substandard writing abilities.

Educators do not need to guess what is vastly underrepresented in so many of the tests used to measure our students. After all, as opposed to monitoring the filling in of little ovals with a number two pencil, it is rather difficult to effectively grade millions of essays.

Limited writing ability, moreover, is truly a small brick in the wall of problems our so-called best students are displaying. Many of these college youngsters, when asked, "What do you think?" crawl into an intellectual fetal position. A weekend requiring at least three hours to complete reading assignments? A frightening number of college freshman cannot comprehend dedicating this much time to homework.

Freshman attending our colleges and universities today are accustomed to proving their academic worth by connecting the dots organized neatly for them within our K–12 classrooms. Further, when instead of being offered an opportunity to color their group project poster for extra credit they are urged to intellectually contribute via writing or speaking, countless of our best and brightest are exposed as victims of the curriculum, assessment, and accountability craze that has come to define current American public education.

Success for K–12 public education has been redefined in this country to meet the demands of those who have never met our students and have completely forgotten what it was that made our grandparents successful. Our students are being so carelessly compared to their peers in China, for example, that we have too often dedicated our classrooms to the answering of difficult test questions and not enough to emphasizing work ethic, interpersonal skills, time management, consistency, sacrifice, and decency. If our nation is ever crippled by the power of China, it will be due to how the Chinese work—not what they know.

There is danger in continuing to emphasize what our students can answer without teaching these young people how to find answers when times are difficult, the value of working at it every day, the effort required to earn what one wants and needs, and the honor of respecting the kid in the next desk. We adults either teach this to the children in our lives or we do not, and it should not remain a mystery to us why our kids thrive, struggle, or otherwise.

Introduction

This book is in response to the pleas for a better student, a more focused and prepared young adult transitioning from the middle and high school years to colleges, the workforce, and beyond. Students, as this book will uncover, reflect the expectations and habits emphasized by the relevant adults in their lives.

Young people today are no better or worse than the youth of forty years ago; today's children have been allowed to develop unimpressive habits—their laziness has been taught. The highly capable students of today are not struggling to read and write effectively in college because school districts have yet to find the perfect high school English curriculum, but rather because parents and teachers have failed to teach young people the value of taking responsibility for life's necessities (like reading and writing well) before enjoying life's benefits.

Too many in education have been teaching children and young adults that benefits are free. Student athletes are applauded for playing three sports, despite carrying an embarrassing grade point average. Student council members are allowed out of class for three straight days to decorate for prom, and then parents clean up the associated mess while their children catch up on sleep. There are pizza parties in some classrooms the day after difficult tests.

Educators do this, perhaps, as an apology for pounding curriculum and assessment upon students without having the necessary time to actually *teach* what must be measured. Most teachers instinctively know that their approach to teaching has been marginalized by the measure-mongers.

In the end, young people model and learn what relevant adults emphasize. Curriculum is retained not because educators test for it; the most impressive students thrive because curriculum has come along for the ride. College-bound students are not learning calculus because they think it is interesting, or because the state tests their math aptitude thrice a year, or because the math teacher attended fourteen workshops aimed at best practices for the teaching of calculus.

The best students learn calculus because their moms, dads, and math teachers are not overly concerned with the fact that these kids dislike solving equations. Furthermore, for these students, going to school and being moderately successful—doing their best—is the price they must pay for playing sports, having a cell phone, driving a car they do not own, and decorating for prom.

So what should educators emphasize, if not the curriculum and how to assess it? This is not answered simply, especially by those who believe school focus should rest upon the "proof" provided by state and national test scores. Emphasis, however, should derive from what it is the responsible and successful public truly wants young people to embody.

When given the opportunity to reflect, the best teachers and parents know what they hope for their youths. If adults—teachers and parents—have done their jobs admirably, today's kids are:

1. Talented and Accomplished
2. Busy and Productive
3. Good

How does this happen? How can school districts increase the percentage of all-state choir participants and full-scholarship Ivy League students who have a knack for being both incredibly busy and productive? What makes a grocery store manager say, "I'd take twenty-five of your kid to work here," while the woman across the street tells her friends that your daughter "could be trusted with anything" related to babysitting?

The most talented, accomplished, busy, productive, and respectful students are not accidents; they are taught to be who and what they are. Furthermore, adequate yearly progress (AYP) prowess and academic scholarships are not a result of prioritizing tests, and young people do not naturally gravitate toward volunteerism, mentoring, and helping the elderly woman from across the street shovel her driveway. These kids become exceptional because the adults in their lives have placed a profound emphasis on doing the right things for the right reasons.

The Wrong Emphasis: Youths Learn What Adults Teach is written in four parts. Part 1, "Where We Are," consists of three chapters examining the current state of K–12 public education and its relationship with our citizenry.

Chapters 1 and 2 expose ugly truths about schools and the public they serve. Chapter 3 addresses the political rhetoric affecting education and what the consequences have been for children, homes, and our nation's teachers.

Part 2, "Blaming the Scale," reveals the flawed methodology used by governmental education experts, outlining how and why public schools have transitioned from teaching children and adolescents to focusing extensively on the measurement of education.

Chapter 4 describes Andrew, a talented and accomplished high school student from the 1990s. What made him a successful student and adolescent, and how was this possible before Core Standards and AYP?

Chapter 5 addresses the consequences facing teachers as they struggle to appropriately educate children for significant success. This question begs for an answer: Are today's teachers being groomed for the role of "classroom secretary" and directed, for better and for worse, to "teach to the test"? Moreover, have parents been duped into allowing schools full ownership of the educational process?

Chapter 6 transitions the text from the scale to what it is young people actually learn (or do not learn) in and out of school. What do people remember from school twenty years after graduating? Aside from our necessities (reading and writing, for example) and what a student may find uniquely interesting (imagine when Bill Gates was first exposed to electronics!), children remember the *unwritten curriculum* great parents and teachers emphasize on a daily basis.

Part 3 of this book, "Great Habits of the Unwritten Curriculum," details the unwritten curriculum all youths deserve to learn for long-term success. Chapter 7 examines the need for our children to think. The current emphasis in education leans heavily in the direction of training students to correctly answer questions. This becomes problematic when life requires thinking. Chapter 8 addresses age-appropriate people and communication skills. ACT score? This is often irrelevant; countless intelligent high school graduates are completely disregarded because they have not learned, among millions of other things, how to shake an adult's hand.

Chapter 9 discusses timeliness and attendance, and the tenth chapter begs the need to teach work ethic and dedication in schools and beyond. Nothing an adult can emphasize is more important than the tenacity to work hard. Not only does work ethic lead to growth, but it is also essential for overcoming struggles—academic and otherwise.

The eleventh chapter emphasizes the need for our youth to learn respect, decency, and humility. What is expected from young people? What is tolerated? Are adolescents praised for touchdowns—or for respecting their classmates? With this, students deserve to learn from responsible adults that there is a significant difference between having a talent and truly having to work at something; humility is learned when people know what they should feel pride in.

Chapter 12, addressing responsibility for self and society, reminds parents and educators that the nation badly needs a generation capable of working with other people to accomplish significant goals. Today's children must learn the value of being reliable and the necessary trust of relying on others as well. Indeed, the need for teamwork must be emphasized while at the same time teaching children that responsible, capable citizens do not look for "someone else" to supply their wants and meet their needs.

Chapter 13 outlines the vitality of teaching children and adolescents perspective. One of the greatest gifts a high school graduate could receive is the feeling that he or she knows next to nothing . . . and a willingness to embrace this reality as a challenge.

The book's conclusion begs educators at all levels to remember that academic and personal growth within schools and communities comes as a result of emphasizing fundamentals (great habits). In many ways, educators and concerned citizens have no choice regarding curriculum, assessment, and accountability; this is how politicians gain office and it is how educational funding will be spent. However, parents and educators can choose to accomplish more, accomplish faster, and accomplish for both short- and long-term success by emphasizing what has been proven to lead to improvement.

The fourteenth and final chapter reminds great educators to use their autonomy. Educators, including administrators, maintain an enormous amount of freedom regarding what is emphasized in school, and pretending that results are attained by focusing on "results before process" has proven to be ineffective.

Likewise, parents are called to recognize the moments they are needed to influence the lives of their children. There is a time for parental passivity (at football games, for example), and there is a time for first-class involvement (insisting upon a high school senior taking a full schedule). Impressive parents have the power to educate with an effectiveness even the best school districts cannot match.

Unfortunately, educational "experts" have too often forgotten what constitutes a successful adult. A nation of kids struggling to read and write at grade level? AYP is developed. Nearly one-third of college freshman enrolled in remedial courses? Common Core standards are established.

High standards and accountability are, of course, necessary for American education, yet we have allowed ourselves to become the out-of-shape man who insists that finding the right scale and a loose pair of pants will equate to losing weight.

If we hope to have more of our children like the most successful of our young people, we would be wise to remember what we (parents and teachers alike) have emphasized with these great students: successful habits.

Part One

Where We Are

ONE
The Ugly Truth

A BRIEF SNAPSHOT

As this sentence is written, public education in the United States is perceived by far too many as a negotiable, only partially relevant nuisance. A frightening percentage of the public views the potential benefits of attending school the same way they view a book given away at a garage sale—something only relevant after other, far more important items have been obtained.

Many citizens within school districts have difficulty hiding the reality that on the list of priorities for their children, success in the classroom ranks somewhere beneath participating (and hopefully winning) in sports, having a really cool cell phone to use during study hall, and enjoying a post-prom party with fantastic prizes.

Unfortunately, as droves of America's young citizens have regressed into a state of "fat, dumb, and happy," the perceptions of too many public schools have evolved, in many cases, into an embarrassment for our communities. This most likely happens for several reasons, and few of them are sensible.

School, after all, is where children spend most of their day. What else could be at fault for these dang kids nowadays? This faulty perception, along with perceived unacceptable test scores across the K–12 spectrum, underwhelming freshman classes throughout our nation's colleges and universities, and a generation of upper twentysomethings moving back home to live with their parents, conveniently leads people to blame the one public entity almost everyone has in common—schools.

What this brief snapshot provides is not actually an image of schools today, for many of the same teachers and administrators working in the nation's "embarrassing" public schools are no worse as educators than those who are beaming about their Core Standard accomplishments and AYP status within America's "best" public schools. The picture needing attention, rather, is that of the public.

Great educators have known for some time now that an alarming percentage of today's public associated with public schools, quite simply, "just don't get it." Any school administrator can tell stories ranging from the unfortunate to the bizarre about their respective citizens. The ideals of a public school are at times at amazing odds with the priorities of moms, dads, and their children.

Public school administrators witness countless head-scratching moments involving students and their parents. Considering that high school students are adolescents, it is easy to understand why and how students can behave poorly. Kids are allowed to display immature behavior now and then; they are kids. When it relates to their forty-five-year-old parents, however, educators are often at a complete loss for understanding.

One administrator met with a mother and father in his office after their son admitted to selling prescription medication to some of his friends at school. This was obviously an incredibly serious situation with equally serious disciplinary actions required; selling drugs brings police officers to meetings such as these, and a suspension from school can quickly become the least of anyone's concerns. The parents of this boy appeared to understand the enormity of the situation at first, but it did not take long for them to veer into the absurd (note: these were college-educated, upper-middle class adults in their forties).

"Will he still be able to play baseball this spring?" This was the first question asked. Their son was about five minutes away from leaving the high school with a police officer, he had admitted to both stealing and selling prescription medication, he was likely using the drugs he was selling, and their chief concern was his eligibility for baseball. This is just one example of the bizarre; public schools are riddled with tales like these.

There is no need to hide and wait for students to peddle drugs in schools to find telling signs of the conflicting agendas of educators and the public. The everyday events, if given consideration, are enough to make great educators and parents pause.

Kids selling drugs? Sometimes. Gang fights? It is possible. Bullying? Of course; we are dealing with kids. These are the conflicts that make the news, but this is not why great teachers and administrators are losing their minds while effective parents struggle to comprehend their daft peers. The reality is, for an alarming number of parents, the education of their children has fallen down the list of priorities—somewhere beneath getting a haircut, playing sports, and having a multitude of tasty lunch options for their choosey children.

Although there are some undeniable exceptions to the rule, most of the stress young people experience (and which causes the low priority of academics) is a result of choices. An assistant principal met with a mother of two high school girls a few years ago; the mother initiated the meeting because she feared the downward spiral both of her daughters were displaying both at home and at school. The girls, one sophomore and one junior, were average, capable students, and both were actively involved with sports.

"I just don't know what to do." Hearing this come from a teary-eyed mother can remind public school officials that some parents have a terrible time seeing the forest for the trees. Her daughters were, quite frankly, living hard. They came to school, they played basketball, they slept very little most nights, they ran themselves ragged on weekends, they had family obligations, and they had friend obligations.

The girls each drove a car to school every day, and they each carried a cell phone. And, to no one's surprise, they were beginning to show signs that they could not keep this pace and be successful in school or at home.

The mother was asked a series of questions.

1. Who pays for your daughters' car insurance?
2. Do the girls have an enforced curfew—even on weekends?
3. Does anyone monitor their cell phone usage?
4. Is basketball something guaranteed to your daughters, or is it an extra, something they can have for fun when they work hard in school?

It was a great conversation. The mother cleared her eyes rather quickly, and this parent and the educator talked about the girls and how they were doing absolutely nothing surprising. These high school girls were simply acting like adolescents; they were living in their version of the fast lane with no plans for rest or reflection. This is what kids will do if adults allow it.

Why has education fallen down our list of priorities? It has happened because adults have allowed it to happen. The woman with the two struggling high school girls had honestly forgotten that she and her husband, not the kids, run their house. Do the girls want to continue driving cars they do not own? Great, here are the minimum GPA standards required for automobile usage within our family.

Cell phone calls at two o'clock in the morning? No phone for a week. Are these rules ridiculous and childish? When we pay our own bills, make our own meals, and are held completely responsible for our behavior, then we can make our own rules.

The absence of this line of thinking has hurt education in America more than any other issue. Kids are not stupid. In fact, they are no different than the children of fifty years ago—with one significant alteration: the children of fifty years ago had adults in their lives who were not obsessed with making their children content in the moment.

OUR GRANDPARENTS

The ill informed and the apathetic have not always been made to feel comfortable as it relates to public education. America's grandparents (and their parents) would have difficulty comprehending some of the remarkable issues parents and teachers face on a daily basis. Blaming schools for the current state of our nation's youth? This is unthinkable for people who were raised generations ago. Hearing grown men and women, completely healthy and financially secure, say about their children, "I just don't know what to do!" would have our elders ashamed of what has become of us.

Why reference grandparents as things relate to education and raising children? The adults of yesteryear were taught differently about the notion of genuine success, and both the adults and children of today can benefit from their perspectives—and how they came to develop their perspectives. If success, whether in life, school, relationships, career, or finances, has any role in the goals of raising children, it is difficult to deny that the people of yesteryear learned more substance in their youth (and in school) than many children are learning now.

Genuine success. This ingredient is precisely what is missing from the education of too many current young people. The number of students who can count on a mom, dad, or grandparents for tough love are dwindling. This is well known, yet the collective parent-and-public-school approach to dealing with the unfortunate reality has been more laissez-faire than proactive.

It is common to hear leaders in K–12 education say something akin to "we cannot control what happens at home, but we can make an amazing difference during the time we have the kids in school." This is undeniable, but educators often miss the point about what, exactly, is happening or not happening within students' homes. The problem is not that moms and dads are stupid people and that American public education must overcome this by providing phenomenal academics; the issue is that too many of them are not raising their kids very well.

The solutions, however, mistakenly revolve around the academic slide today's young people have been displaying. Educators are often dismayed by what students do not know or cannot do by certain grade levels, so efforts are doubled with curriculum planning and assessment strategies to boost the struggling youngsters. These strategies work within some school districts and have accomplished very little in others. Why?

School districts accomplishing impressive academic turnarounds are not benefiting from a nifty new assessment plan to measure their overhauled curriculum, for it is being shown in this country that the community down the road can be using the same curriculum while continuing to struggle.

Successful schools are improving their performances largely because the administrators and teachers are starting to behave like bothered moms, dads, and grandparents. They have grown tired of waiting for someone else to do the job of preparing young people for responsible adulthood, so they are doing it themselves with no apologies.

THE NEW JOB DESCRIPTION OF TEACHERS

Tough love may be something that moms and dads reference periodically, but aside from those who suffer from great economic stress, most of the nation's youth are perilously wading through childhood and adolescence expecting their creature comforts without learning enough about the necessary discipline and sacrifice required to afford such pleasantries. Discipline and sacrifice are taught by adults who are not afraid to upset children now and then—this is tough love.

This reality has become increasingly absent from public schools and has unfortunately symbolized the mistakes adults are making with our children and adolescents. Educators and parents too frequently promote and ensure athletics, for example, while at the same time countless student athletes struggle to meet established academic or behavior standards. Prom has become an epic drama within many high schools, and every year across the country thousands of students who struggled to attend school with any sort of regularity are guaranteed a life-changing prom experience.

Somewhere along the line, countless moms and dads stopped fighting with their children. It has become much easier for some parents to simply "get along" with their kids, especially if they are not finding significant trouble. Educators have too often followed that lead. Billy and Suzie have missed a lot of school this year, certainly, but they are such nice kids after all—and it doesn't seem to hurt anyone if Billy and Suzie attend the prom, does it?

This is short-term thinking. It leads to the aura of entitlement today's children have developed, and it is what Billy and Suzie are learning if the results of adult decisions resemble this situation. Moreover, this is what students will remember. Long after calculus and the capital of Peru have been forgotten, Billy and Suzie will still be thinking that good things in life should be guaranteed despite not having earned such pleasantries.

Effective parents and educators have been fighting this trend. While the nation and the collective states have scrambled to develop the best curriculum-and-assessment programs needed for the challenges ahead, the best have been quietly adjusting their job descriptions to include that which is missing from the lives of too many youths. "Getting along" with young people is great, but it cannot come at the cost of educating a generation of young people primed to fail before every challenge.

The students and parents forty or fifty years ago did not need to be counseled to understand that skipping school for a haircut was inappropriate. Unfortunately, that counseling has become one of the public school job descriptions—and no assessment strategy can accomplish this. Great educators merely dip their toes in the pool of curriculum and assessment, and effective parents seldom make their child's short-term happiness the priority; they both dive into the deep end of what is best for the children.

There are lessons to be learned in today's schools, and although safety, happiness, and self-worth are vital, they cannot come at the price of hard work. Sometimes students need to struggle with the process of working at something. An educator's career is about teaching young people to overcome their difficulties, whether the problems are based in math class, on the football field, or in the cafeteria. Too many students are learning, instead, how to avoid discomfort until someone else solves the problem.

There is a place for some "old school" renaissance in public education. It is not as though we need to dream of what it would be like to graduate students who have worked their tails off in the classroom. Great teachers are already accomplishing this with their students, and the results are available for anyone willing to examine them. For example, any college professor can share that when he or she asks students how or why they became skilled writers, one of two answers is provided:

1. The parents played a huge role in the development of reading and writing.
2. There was a high school English teacher that consistently demanded more from them.

Amazingly, we have somehow glossed over these great teachers who possess a disdain for mediocrity. We pass it off as though it is a coincidence that their students are better behaved, better test-takers, and better prepared for the challenges beyond high school. We say things like, "Oh, that Mr. Arvidson. He can get grumpy sometimes. But he sure has a way with those kids." Yes, this "way" he has with kids is called good teaching.

Teachers like Mr. Arvidson have sat through all of the daylong workshops on standards-based teaching and common assessment strategies. These great teachers, further, have likely used the information they have attained to bolster their successes in the classroom. Here is what leaders in public education either fail to realize or refuse to acknowledge, however: five years from now, when the current approaches to curriculum delivery and student assessment have been determined inadequate and are replaced by newer, fresher "systems," the best teachers will still have their "way."

In the most dynamic classrooms, curriculum attainment is something that happens by accident. Success, according to the best teachers in a school district, is not reflected by the charts and graphs of a NAEP test. Rather, success for these great educators is found in the process. Students in Mr. Arvidson's class are not exposed to superior academic philosophies or advanced curriculum developed by government specialists; they are exposed to the tremendous enthusiasm, work ethic, expectations, and insights of Mr. Arvidson.

Successful students have learned to work hard. This, more than anything else, is what separates great schools from our adequate schools. Academics? Why would educators assume that academic success can be attained via any strategy aside from the process of diligent work? Successful adults should all know better than that. In fact, Mr. Arvidson's students have proven that nearly any curriculum-and-assessment theory can be effective if the proper mentality accompanies it.

The best teachers are not naïve enough to believe that the curriculum provided in their classrooms will be remembered forever. Children grow up, and unless they continue to focus on specific academic endeavors, they forget the rhyme scheme of a Shakespearean sonnet, the name of France's leader during World War II, and how to identify the pancreas in a dissected pig. This does not bother great educators.

So what is failure for teachers like these? Students in Mr. Arvidson's class fail when they stop working. Class grades, GPAs, ACT scores, and MAP test results are nothing more than symptoms of doing other, far more important things well for great teachers. Students react well to teachers who think like this because it almost always pays off.

Results? Results are what happen after the work has been completed. Further, results, at their core, are more about the work itself than the number reflected on the final test. This was good teaching fifty years ago, it is good teaching now, and it will be good teaching in 2050.

The best public school teachers are nothing short of amazing, for they are successful at challenging students to work outside of a previous comfort zone. English students read and write beyond their previous abilities, math students solve equations that would have befuddled them in the past, and science students conduct experiments they could not imagine before they entered Mr. Arvidson's class.

Further, these teachers somehow establish an incredible rapport with their students to assure them they are not only safe while working diligently, but that their efforts can be both fun and rewarding.

The ugliest of truths, at least within the perspective of educational leaders, is the reality that leaders within education too often struggle to recognize the best teachers. The consequence for this lack of vision is endlessly significant: we continue to search for solutions to a declining state of education—or youth accomplishment—in this country while the people who should be consulted are just down the hall. They are either teaching students seven periods a day, or they are raising their own children to accomplish tremendous feats. Many of these adults go remarkably unnoticed.

TWO
Cultural Responsibility

IT TAKES A VILLAGE?

A high school administrator from a small town in Minnesota was called on to work with faculty, staff, students, and the community in order to have the educational process run as smoothly as possible. There were obviously challenges to this job, and not the least of these was the fact that, because of issues with the school budget and limited available space for a growing number of students, the high school consisted of every student in grades seven through twelve.

This situation was far from ideal, for most educators agree that students of a certain age (seventh and eighth graders, for example) are better served by a middle school atmosphere, apart from older students and their associated realities.

Upon accepting such a position, with the responsibility of maintaining peace and sanity among thirteen-year-old children and their eighteen-year-old schoolmates, an administrator should expect the obvious concerns of hallway duty, lunchtime supervision (this is when seventh-grade loudmouths get stuffed in lockers), and providing a school climate appropriate for all ages. Some issues related to children are predictable; these challenges are a daily process throughout any principal's tenure.

What is far more difficult to predict, however, is the enormity of negative outside influence students drag into school on a daily basis from the parts of their lives teachers and responsible citizens can neither control nor comprehend.

A meeting was scheduled to discuss a plan of action for two students. One student, a seventh-grade girl, was already enrolled in the building, and the other, a sixth-grade boy, would be enrolled the following year. The meeting was attended by the high school administrators, the director of special education (both students received services), families of both students, and two representatives from social services.

The school provided hot coffee (one man was given a soda) and a tray of cookies, and it was made certain everyone was provided with a comfortable chair. What could possibly cause over fifteen pleasant, nonargumentative people to fill a conference room regarding students more than three years away from driving a car?

The girl was impregnated by the boy, and, for one reason or another, she miscarried. The story could end here, and it would be enough to make us all uneasy. Innocence lost and potential lifelong consequences are enough to make any reasonable person, educator or not, saddened by what is happening to some kids in this country. Unfortunately, this story takes an unbelievable turn for the worse.

The purpose for the meeting was so district employees could ensure a reasonable level of separation between the two children during the school day. Obviously, the boy and girl were behaving inappropriately, and a strong presence of supervision would be necessary to assure the students' families nothing unpleasant would happen during school hours.

Obviously, despite the fact that unthinkable adult realities had confronted these two kids and their respective families, all adults involved were well aware that they were dealing with children. Obviously, everyone understood the enormity of the situation requiring the presence of two families, all relevant school district administrators, and a small team of social service representatives. Right?

Wrong. Instead, less than five minutes into the meeting, the school district personnel and social service workers were struck dumbfounded by what came from the mouths of the families. With the support of both families, the girl's grandmother looked across the table and assured school officials there was no need to worry about keeping the two children separated.

"We lost the baby. So Daniel is moving in with us to try again." The room was silent for a moment. There was absolutely no possible way everyone heard what they thought they heard.

"Excuse me?" It was explained with great detail that the tragedy of losing their baby via a miscarriage will not hold this young couple down. The boy, a sixth grader, would now be living with the seventh-grade girl and her family. The conflict, at least according to the moms, dads, and grandparents, was solved. Pass the cookies, please.

At this point, the role of school administration became nearly insignificant. Thankfully, social service agents immediately took control of the situation. In fact, the families involved were asked to leave the high school and relocate for what was obviously an unforeseen and ill-advised solution to an already tragic chain of events.

The boy and the girl continued to attend school together; furthermore, despite the proclamation from social services (and the associated cooperation from school administrators) to have the two children separated as much as possible during school hours, these kids likely found ways every day to ignore this advisement.

It is difficult for noneducators to imagine caring for the children of others by attempting to protect these children from their own families. Seriously, a sixth-grade boy and seventh-grade girl living together as a couple? It may sound unbelievable, but educators see this level of stupidity from their villagers more often than can be comprehended by rational adults.

This is the humanity educators are asked to mold into responsible young adults. It may very well take a village to raise a child, but great teachers throughout America have been wondering for quite some time now why they are expected to fill the role of "village parent," while no one seems to place any responsibilities or consequences on the laziest or most misguided citizens.

The "it takes a village" mantra was made famous by Hilary Clinton, and the words are not by themselves a misguided thought. The concept, as it relates to education, is well intended, especially if the bulk of the citizens have committed to making their children (and their village) exceptional.

Impressive parents and educators know better, however. America's villages consist of everyone; there are the exceptional, the leaders, the silent majority, the followers, the disrespectful, and somehow the people who believe it is prudent for preteen children to make babies.

Applying the "it takes a village" philosophy to public education in this country exposes some realities about our communities and the daunting task educators and willing parents are given in trying to educate children.

To begin, our villages (the communities within our country) appear to have a fair share of the ill informed and ill willed. This, of course, does not make us different than any other country, yet we now find ourselves suffering at the hands of idiocy more than ever before in America. One need not look any further than the story of two children and their respective families working to annihilate the innocence of childhood while using school as nothing more than a comfortable place to have a hot cup of coffee, a few tasty cookies, and a hangout for two kids in love.

Yet public educators are not in a position to recruit their students and certainly not their students' families. Teachers are charged with teaching and mentoring those who walk through the front door; they are charged with making the village better than it was yesterday by asking more from all children today.

Understandably, the best people—educators and parents—have grown tired of arguing with the ill informed and ill willed. Why? In the end, their words are measured to be nothing but an opinion. If an educator's job is to take children where they are, regardless of where they are, and have them work toward AYP and Core Standards, an enormous problem for public schools has been exposed: children clearly need more than AYP and Core Standard excellence; furthermore, their unmet needs are making genuine academic achievement nothing short of a pipe dream.

The best people are losing their patience. Those in education know this because the numbers are booming in charter schools, home schooling, and private school enrollment—all of this despite a failing economy. Meanwhile, public educators continue to bend over backward, trying desperately not to offend the noisemakers within the villages.

Further, public school officials struggle to comprehend how it is possible that their efforts never seem to please the very people they placate. What does this tell us? Over time, leaders in education have made the mistake of allowing the village idiots to have influence on our educational processes.

A great portion of effective teaching, clearly, is to provide an academic base from which young people can progress into adulthood. But the nation's schools are not failing AYP because American children are stupid; we are failing our tests (and subsequently seeking magical programs to fix everything) because too many of the villagers do not care enough (or appropriately) about raising their children. For far too many people in society, the concept of "it takes a village" has meant "it is the job of someone else" to do that which is not easy.

Solutions to this accepted trend will not be simple. The village needs to be educated. Citizens are necessary for great public education for children, but the ignorant and malcontent cannot be tolerated as decision makers. Until great parents and educational leaders in the United States take control of schools (and the associated expectations of students and their families), the performance of public schools will be at the mercy of those with the strongest personalities and loudest voices.

Step one, perhaps, is to make certain great educators and parents possess the loudest voices when it comes to education. If, in fact, it takes a village, perhaps educators and capable citizens must evolve into something stronger than what they have been in the past. The nation's schools are not coffee shops, and students and their families are not customers.

The relationship with students and the public is endlessly more important and complicated than the reactionary mode utilized while attempting to make everyone happy with the school and its product. Educational leaders and strong parents know what is best for students, and sometimes what is best for students is not popular with everyone in the village.

CUSTOMER SERVICE

Whether it is because of the popularity of private schools and their reputed academic and behavioral expectations, the fact that the public school just down the road has an excellent athletic tradition, or a simple fear of disappointing the crazies among us, countless school administrators in America have made a habit of wooing the students and families the way business owners seek to please the customers.

Too many public school officials fear that if students are not provided with what mom and dad have deemed essential, the kids will enroll elsewhere. This would not necessarily be the worst situation for the teaching profession, except for the fact that the list of "essentials" is too often grossly unrelated to anything and everything today's children actually need in school.

Academic excellence? Droves of parents do not meet with building principals to discuss a school's academic integrity. They do, however, sign petitions to increase the high school lunch fast-food offerings for their hungry adolescent children. Help out with the school district anti-drug policy? Some folks are willing, of course, but never as many as the number of people who will meet with an activity director to discuss the discouraging results of the football team.

Leaders in education have found themselves appeasing these people and their often ridiculous concerns. Subway in the lunch line? Fine. A special school board meeting to talk about the "struggling" football coach, the same man who was skilled enough to go undefeated five years ago? Fine. Miss twenty-five days of school and still expect to attend the prom? Fine.

Meanwhile, the issues of academic rigor, work ethic, attendance, respect, and decency, and the overarching process of teaching young people to better themselves, have become what educational leaders discuss in the quiet of their own offices. But students are always learning something, and it is frightening to think about what adults are teaching young people when they fail to stand and deliver necessary but uncomfortable realities.

This trend is hurting schools, students, and communities. Public schools must stop resembling the Holiday Inn. Educators are not here to make everyone happy—especially if that temporary satisfaction contradicts the purpose. Education is an entirely different enterprise; students and their families are not customers, and they are most definitely not always right.

Ironically, most businessmen do not tolerate from their customers what educators have grown to accept from the misguided public. Teachers are servers; they spend long, hard hours doing difficult work (that few people could do well) for lower-middle-class money.

This approach, ironically, has made the job of teaching more difficult—and it has made educators less respected as professionals. Transitioning from a K–12 career to higher education provided one educator with an experience that has moved him to rethink leadership within the field of education.

Becoming an education professor meant moving his family. This, of course, required packing up one house and unloading everything in another. During this process, he found himself far short on boxes. On a hunch, he tried Walmart at midnight. His plan seemed flawless. There were probably no more than three customers in the store at the time, and a truck had just delivered new merchandise to be unloaded and stocked.

There were boxes of all shapes and sizes everywhere throughout the nearly deserted store. The problem was, the boxes were not available—not yet. After seeing various boxes he needed for packing up the kitchen, the moving educator asked to speak to the store manager. His intention with this conversation was nothing more than to have her understand that he was not stealing merchandise; he would just be taking the boxes. The conversation, however, put a wrinkle in his plans.

"You can't have these boxes until 1:00 a.m."

"Seriously?" The teacher tried his best to avoid sounding disrespectful and rude, but he questioned why he could not, at midnight, take some empty boxes home to continue a horrible night of packing up the kitchen. After all, what is the difference between midnight and one in the morning? Will there be a wave of folks flying through the doors at one wanting free boxes?

The man was tired, grumpy, and dirty, and he was absolutely not in the mood to go back home and return in one hour for what he needed in the moment. The manager appeared to understand the educator's dilemma, but this did not change her policy.

"This is how things work here, sir." And that was it. The Walmart night-shift manager looked him straight in the eyes and without apology let him know, without feeling obligated to share the reasoning, that empty cardboard boxes do not leave her store before she wants them to leave.

"This is how things work here, sir." What a fantastic answer. So much for "the customer is always right." In fact, sometimes it is better for people to not get what they want. Sometimes we can learn a few things after being disappointed.

At one sharp, the teacher presented himself, tired and still somewhat bothered, to the night manager. She was all smiles. He was further befuddled when she gave him anything and everything he needed related to boxes.

"Hey, you, we have some really strong boxes over here. . . . These hold tons of paper, so they are big and thick." She grabbed a shopping cart for each of them and whisked him around her store at about twice the speed the tired man wanted to move. She asked him where he was moving, if he had sold his house yet, and if he had ever been in Walmart this late before. Although the man was still tired, he could not possibly remain angry at this woman who was helping him with everything he asked for and beyond.

The two of them filled their shopping carts with broken-down boxes. One of their last stops within the store was near another employee, who was busy stocking shelves. The boxes she had emptied earlier were neatly broken down and stacked on the floor. The manager and this woman rummaged through these looking for a smaller box size, something good for "the kitchen drawer" every respectable home must have. After finding a few of this size, the manager and the teacher started heading elsewhere, but not before the woman took time to speak two words to her manager. "Thank you," was all she spoke.

Why the thanks? The manager explained that it had actually been common for people to come into the store on truck nights and ask for boxes. Unfortunately, many of those requesting boxes were unwilling to wait for the night staff to get them emptied. This led to people literally emptying boxes of merchandise on the floor, leaving messes for the staff to clean up and shelve.

The manager was very new to her position. When she began as a supervisor, she met with her staff and asked what it was they needed from her. Along with a few other concerns, the night staff at Walmart begged that they have more time available to them for stocking the shelves without customers at their heels. Quite obviously, this manager found a way to honor that request, and her staff appeared to be appreciative.

More than a few connections can be made between the realities confronting the nation's schools and the story shared here. To begin, sometimes the experts need to act like experts. The man's need for boxes was very important—to him. The Walmart night manager, however, could see the bigger picture.

Customer service? Yes, it is important, but not at the cost of confusing right versus wrong. Furthermore, there was no real danger of Walmart losing any customers that night, despite the fact that a sleepy educator spent an hour displeased.

Leaders in education can learn from this woman. Educators should ask themselves who they are championing. Are we looking out for those like the midnight crew at Walmart, only asking to be respected enough to do their jobs without cleaning up the messes of the impatient? Or are we looking out for what too many show themselves to be, an insensitive and incredibly intolerant person?

The people who have left public schools for private, charter, and home schools are not necessarily the angry noisemakers; they are often the quiet, thoughtful folks who are disgusted that the angry noisemakers are being appeased. If great parents and public educators desire to do the right things for the right reasons, they need to be willing to rest easily when some people become angry.

Superintendents, principals, and activities directors would be wise to follow the night manager's approach as it pertains to leading a staff and respectfully leading a community with an issue as important as education.

Instead of worrying about student and respective family upheaval coming from having too few tasty lunchroom choices, the cell phone policy, or a football team that cannot seem to win two games in a row, leaders in public education must begin to look these people in the eyes and, with steadfast resolve, tell them there are bigger problems needing attention.

When we act like leaders, it is not only likely that the noisemakers leveling one threat or another will fail to follow through and eventually shut up (complaining and acting are two entirely different realities), but we will also make great strides toward impressing the people we should be seeking to impress.

THREE
Political Rhetoric

"In politics we presume that everyone who knows how to get votes knows how to administer a city or a state. When we are ill, we do not ask for the handsomest physician, or the most eloquent one." —Plato

LOSING PERSPECTIVE

We are fortunate beyond our understanding in this country; we are allowed to choose our leaders and either sing their praises or scream their shortcomings. American educators, as much or more than any group of professionals, furthermore, have exercised their political freedom by leaving no doubt whatsoever where their allegiances lie. Yet Plato's quote above about politics almost perfectly explains the ironic disappointment many American educators experience as they apply political rhetoric to the realities of public teaching.

How can political allegiances and activism be anything but beneficial for teachers and education-friendly parents? It happens because the game of politics has a way of creating shortsighted thinking from otherwise incredibly intelligent and talented adults. Educators often forget that the issue of education is typically one of a dozen hot topics candidates must address in this country as they woo their voters; furthermore, public education is almost always trivialized into a few canned, preordained talking points.

Despite agreeing on nothing else associated with public education, Democrats and Republicans somehow come together to determine what will be their source of conflict—and what neither party will dare to address with full candor:

- Funding
- Academic standards

- School, teacher, and student assessments and accountability

And their cleverest approach:

- Ignoring the concept of public responsibility for public education

This is the beginning of where even the best education-friendly adults lose their perspective. The "game," as defined by the major political parties, comes in prepackaged issues. Public school supporters, the same adults who work wonders with children on a daily basis despite hundreds of societal issues working against them, turn themselves into torchbearers for their preferred party.

Miraculously, they forget about the vitality of parents reading to their children, the undeniable benefit for kids with two loving parents, the misery drugs are creating for young people, teenage pregnancy, gangs, the benefits of extra curricular activities, proper nutrition, going to bed at a reasonable time, doing homework, or anything else politicians could emphasize at their podiums if they were not too busy narrowing the conversation to funding, academic standards, assessments, and holding everyone accountable.

THE REALITY OF FUNDING

If an educator works long enough, he or she will likely teach throughout the terms of several presidents and state governors. Many will live and work in both traditionally liberal and traditionally conservative states, places where elected officials began their careers as professional wrestlers, comedians, or, as is rather common in America, sons of incredibly wealthy businessmen.

During a teacher's career, however, strikingly little will have changed in the classroom and the associated schools aside from new policies designed to fix everything. Outcome-based education (OBE), for example, has transitioned to state standards; state standards have evolved into the Profile of Learning; and Common Core standards has become the new trend throughout the nation.

Response-to-intervention (RTI) strategies are now commonplace within school districts actively striving to improve students' academic performance and retention. The current national measuring stick, of course, has become AYP. School leaders are deeply engrossed in the goal of achieving annual yearly progress.

This, it seems, is where the funding goes. Educators and education-friendly parents are often too busy teaching and parenting to recognize that Republicans and Democrats are truly interchangeable when it comes to often-wasteful educational funding. If pushed to clarify, many of the best teachers in Minnesota (as an example) would struggle to differentiate between OBE, the Minnesota Graduation Standards, the Profile of Learning, and Core Standards.

The current approach to accomplishing nationwide, across-the-board educational excellence is truly no different than providing millions of people with a superb grocery list and expecting everyone to become great chefs. We know better than this. Yet, somehow, we are asked to believe that government-funded high standards will improve teachers and further student accomplishments. Great teachers, with the help of great parents, make great educational theories work, but it will never work in reverse.

There are two guarantees about public education funding as it relates to our politicians:

1. There will be newly elected public officials in the coming years, and they will have promised a wonderful new (and incredibly expensive) program to improve American education.
2. Their new program will be necessary because the program needing to be replaced (various graduation standards across the nation) completely failed to address both the necessity for great teachers and the responsibilities of citizens regarding the education of children.

Public education idealists often find it difficult to recognize the double standard politicians employ. Voters forget the promises made a few years ago, those glowing words aimed at fixing public education. They are asked to remember, however, the "reasons" educational nirvana has not been realized.

Quite simply, concerned citizens are asked to believe that all that is good in schools is due to the nifty new programs and strategies implemented, and all that has not been remedied can be blamed on the other political party. Evidently, it is just easier to stop thinking sometimes.

POLITICAL BLINDERS

The cover of the fall 2011 *NEA Today* displays a female high school English teacher with folded arms and a stare that must paralyze even her most unruly students. What has this young woman looking so serious? Is she tackling adolescent drug abuse? Teenage pregnancy? Has this teacher reached the end of her tolerance for bullying? Considering her role as an English teacher, is she tired of graduating young people who seemingly cannot fulfill the writing expectations for freshman in colleges and universities?

No, her school must have those issues covered. Her fire burns for politics. The title for the associated article simply reads, "Elections Matter," and the subtitle urges readers to join this focused teacher "in the fight to save students' futures." My goodness, how are we to save the future of our students? The article walks NEA members through the process step-by-step.

To begin, teachers are reminded by the *NEA Today* that conservative Republicans across this great land are ruining public education by drastically and irresponsibly cutting educational funding. A few paragraphs are dedicated for elaboration on this point; three governors, for example, are on record for launching "big-business-funded" assaults on teachers (and on children) via tactics that even make some of their fellow Republicans blush.

The article continues with phase two, a four-step approach to "make a difference in the lives of your public school students, their families, and your own." The first two steps lead to the power hitters of the article, and the advice is almost too amazing to be true.

Public school teachers are not only urged to raise money for Democrats, they are asked to volunteer (presumably with all of their extra time) for these candidates as well. Democrats, of course, are standing by and waiting for our votes (and money, it seems), for the American public school system is only one great election away from educational perfection.

An article like this cannot come as a surprise to anyone, considering its source. If the NEA is not openly cheerleading for the Democratic Party, the sun rises in the west. It is not surprising that teachers' unions prefer Democrats, or even that magazines like *NEA Today* are propaganda machines for the party of their choice. It is almost unbelievable, however, that a nation of teachers (at least as represented and characterized by their unions) and millions of education-friendly parents somehow believe the rhetoric.

Here is the political logic as served by the NEA: Schools need funding. Democrats provide funding. Funding is the difference in public education; therefore, anyone who teaches for a living (or anyone who knows a child) would be completely insane to vote for anyone other than the Democrat *NEA Today* has endorsed. . . . Whew, this sermon sounds great—pass the Kool-Aid.

Is there some truth to the typical public education political rhetoric? Of course. As a whole, Democrats are responsible for more funding directed toward public schools. In fact, this truth is evident to the point that Republicans do not dare even deny it.

With this, as far as public education in the United States is concerned, the Republican Party is almost too misguided to take seriously. School choice as the reasonable and realistic educational option for all American children, even our inner-city kids? Republicans. Reduced funding for school districts falling short with AYP? Republicans. Totally conceding to Democrats the vote of public educators and, therefore, pandering for the votes of the unbelievably ill informed, the antiteacher, the anti-anything-associated-with-unions crowd? Republicans.

The problem with the *NEA Today* article and the droves of teachers who subscribe to the philosophies provided by it is not that they are on the wrong side. The problem is that many within public education have chosen a team that has done absolutely nothing for the profession simply because they cannot fathom joining the team that does not say nice things about public schools. The problem is, as educational politics in America is concerned, there is no right side.

In recent United States history, few professionals (or people as a whole) have been so profoundly satisfied with such a pathetic political effort as is commonly provided by elected Democrats toward public educators. Teachers in this country have become the easiest vote to earn, and we are treated like it.

Completely "buying in" to educational politics, regardless of one's preferred slant, leads to our politicians having little or no interest in addressing the most important needs facing both public education and the nation's youth. The consequences of a nation full of teachers and education-friendly parents actually believing the rhetoric is difficult to comprehend.

Does any truly informed citizen honestly believe the biggest issues surrounding education depend on elected officials and their respective political parties? Teachers spend time with children, they see how some students in school become incredibly successful while others struggle to graduate. Was the successful kid sitting in the more expensive desk? Was the struggling student not exposed to the same curriculum as the thriving student? We know better.

What if there were no Democrats? In a country with no Democrats, provided they were replaced with a different political party, Republicans would be forced to actually try harder to earn the "education vote." The issue with Republicans is not about hating kids or schools or teachers or even about spending too much money. It is about gathering votes.

The Democrats have the votes associated with public education, and the Republicans are forced to collect their votes elsewhere—and that sometimes means belittling public education. Without Democrats, at what point would elected Republicans understand that great public schools are necessary for a great public? Of course, Republicans already know this; they simply cannot gain office by saying it.

And what if there were no Republicans? In a country with no Republicans, Democrats would be forced to actually deliver on their promises. Funding? The NEA can dream of a government full of Democrats ensuring every child has a gold-plated laptop, recliners in their study halls, and two free meals a day, but what would happen when we come to realize that we still have a nation full of children struggling in school and subsequently failing in life after school?

Without Republicans, a major scapegoat for public educational setbacks would be gone. Do any experienced educators truly believe this would fix our educational woes? At what point would elected Democrats have the nerve to tell citizens the truth about whose job it is to raise kids in this country? When would Democrats be willing to face teachers' unions and speak against the retention of substandard teachers?

Education in America is endlessly more complicated than what politicians are willing to communicate. There is little doubt America's elected officials know and believe more than they are willing to say. What would happen to politicians in this country who truly said what they were thinking about the well-being of our children?

Imagine elected officials standing before the television cameras and asking parents to get off their cell phones and read to their children, to stop caring more about sports than academics, to stop blaming the world for how their children turn out. Imagine politicians setting out to make teachers' salaries more competitive within our society by demanding more education, more effort, and more talent from future teachers.

Imagine a president with the guts to say that if countless college students every year can attain a teaching degree as their "fall-back option," it is obviously way too easy to become a teacher in the greatest country in the world. This is what nearly every politician in America really thinks. It is never said because they prefer to avoid becoming former politicians.

Because of this, politicians in this country have divided the voters into groups, convinced most people to focus on a few pet issues (issues they have created), and then gracefully blamed educational failure on either the "other" party or the people who vote for that party.

Meanwhile, caring citizens keep voting and somehow never seem to mind that promises are almost never delivered. Furthermore, until educators and parents have the courage to demand more from their favorite politicians than catchy slogans, promising speeches, and fractionally better funding than the other option, and until politicians demand more from below-average teachers and society as a whole, elections most certainly do not matter.

Public educators, however, do matter. Theirs has become the job of, among a million other things, telling uncomfortable truths to our citizens. As this sentence is being written, my son is in third grade. His teacher sends a minimum of one email a day to parents. She effectively communicates what is being taught in class, the homework expectations for the evening, and what is scheduled for the following day. She also sends separate emails to parents who either deserve or need to hear "other" messages—my son has already endured a few chats about the contents of these "other" emails.

Although it is clear that some parents are contacted about unfinished homework, poor performances on spelling tests, and other issues associated with academics, the messages sent to our home involve my son's incessant need to stick his nose in others' business. If left unchecked, this behavior of his will lead to either a classmate (literally) or a teacher (metaphorically) beating him soundly. His teacher knows this, she cares enough to do the right thing, and she does not apologize for being right.

This is holding families accountable. It is teaching. This is part of the job for today's great educators, and she does not shy away from the responsibility. It takes the courage most politicians lack. Her political affiliation? Nothing could be more irrelevant.

Part Two

Blaming the Scale

FOUR
Andrew, 1990s

GRADUATION STANDARDS

In the early and mid-1990s, the Minnesota Department of Children, Families, and Learning, teaming up with the legislature and the soon-to-be-defunct state board of education, redefined its purpose by creating statewide graduation standards aimed at providing a baseline of knowledge required for citizens to succeed in a *literate society*.

The result of these efforts came to be known as the Minnesota Graduation Standards; high school graduates were required to pass a basic skills test and prove competence within the parameters of the state's Profile of Learning. The Profile of Learning consisted of ten learning areas, and several specific content standards were assigned to each of these areas. Graduating students in Minnesota would be required to complete twenty-four of twenty-eight content standards throughout high school.

Despite the reality that most school districts were granted an extension to manage the overhaul of their K–12 curriculum, the Minnesota Graduation Standards were implemented in 1998. New positions were created in schools across the state; suddenly, there was a strong need for a "curriculum coordinator," a position likely filled by a teacher willing (or begging, perhaps) to leave the classroom for the purposes of assisting colleagues with aligning school curriculum with state standards and coordinating the multitude of test dates within the school district.

Although frustrated, annoyed, and often angry, many teachers in Minnesota were assured their efforts would not be wasted, for like them or not, the standards were "here to stay."

MEANWHILE...

Andrew Atchison was a high school student in Minnesota while his teachers were bracing for the upcoming storm of graduation standards. Although his English, math, and science instructors were certainly aware of the changes headed their way, Andrew was nearly oblivious to that fact. He would graduate from high school and be a successful college student before he either benefited from any significant alterations to the curriculum or completed any of the twenty-eight content standards designed for his cultural and societal literacy.

It is difficult to assess what Andrew missed by graduating before the implementation of state standards. Less confusing, however, is the undeniable truth surrounding his abilities, accomplishments, and character as a high school student.

Andrew was a model student. Although certainly not a genius, he displayed an impressive intellect with a fantastic GPA. Clearly not headed for an arts or athletic scholarship, he nonetheless participated in band, choir, and sports. He was popular in school among both peers and teachers, he displayed leadership skills both formally (student government) and informally (classrooms, hallways, lunch room, etc.), and, perhaps as important as any of his traits, he had fun in school.

Fun? Is there room for fun in school? This, of course, depends on one's definition of fun. While studying Shakespeare's *Macbeth* in his high school World Literature course, Andrew was overcome by a moment and found himself completely incapable of remaining silent.

In Shakespeare's *Macbeth*, the protagonist begs three mysterious and comical witches to reveal the future as it relates to his lineage. The ambitious and tragically insecure king fears the throne will belong to another family, and his angst is justified when the witches produce a fantastical image of countless kings bearing the resemblance of Macbeth's rival, Banquo—thus showing Macbeth a future with a fruitless crown. As part of the revelation process, the witches utilize a large mirror for the purpose of displaying a nearly endless line of royalty stemming from Banquo's offspring.

"Mr. Tufte! I'm sorry, I just have to tell this story!" Before he could be stopped, Andrew was standing and speaking to the entire class. He went on to talk about his recent choir trip to Minneapolis (a significant trip for an outstate Minnesota kid); specifically, there was a great moment he had in an elevator with three beautiful girls.

This is where educators across the country know enough to pull the plug. Stories that begin like this one do not see the finish line in an effective teacher's classroom, right? Andrew was cut off with vigor, and he immediately understood why a story like this should not find the light of day in a high school English classroom. This did not stop him, however. Respectfully and carefully, he insisted.

"Ok, I know this sounds bad, but it's not!" The English teacher held his breath as Andrew continued. He went on to explain that upon receiving his hotel room assignment, he entered the elevator in the lobby only to find himself shoulder to shoulder with these three fetching girls who were also involved in choir. (The English teacher was now considering resignation.)

He was dumbfounded. There he was in the presence of beauty, and he had absolutely nothing to say. Instead, he stared forward at the elevator door—and noticed the entire elevator was wrapped in mirrors. What he saw as he aimed his gaze forward was an endless line of himself and the three young ladies.

So what did he say to these girls? How did he make a winning impression? His fellow World Literature students were in the palm of his hands as he unraveled his tale. To be honest, so was his teacher.

"Hey, this is like *Macbeth*! You know? I mean, we are like the endless line of Banquo's sons, and Macbeth freaks out because he doesn't want to see it . . . umm . . ." The class was on the floor laughing. "I have the chance of a lifetime to be cool, and all I can talk about with these babes is a scene from *Macbeth*!"

Another boy from across the room wondered aloud, "You didn't call them the witches, did you?" The high school juniors and seniors were wiping tears of joy from their eyes and off their desks on a day designated for a comparison of Shakespeare's comedies and tragedies. The interruption to class lasted no more than a few minutes, and fifteen years later it is remembered like it was yesterday.

His ability to apply William Shakespeare to life outside of the English classroom aside, Andrew was the kid we want our students to resemble. How do children transition into adolescence and young adulthood with ability and confidence enough to both reference a Shakespearean play to strangers and make fun of one's self upon returning to safe ground?

Two years earlier, when Andrew was a sophomore, he was slightly more anonymous as a student in a grammar and composition course. Even at this age, however, he displayed characteristics needed to thrive: intelligence, curiosity, work ethic, and confidence. It takes courage, for example, to raise a hand and ask, "What's a gerund, Mr. Tufte? The grammar book has something about it, but it just doesn't make sense to me." Sophomore boys do not typically inquire about gerunds, especially when the current lesson has nothing whatsoever to do with gerunds.

Any educator reading this book recognizes this brand of student. Most public schools have several Andrew Atchisons (and the female equivalents) enrolled. Young people like these are not necessarily rare to the point of attending Mensa meetings on the weekends; they are reasonably intelligent, active, and character-filled kids. They are, however, becoming rarer.

Students like these become educational reference points. If only more students behaved like Andy! Why cannot more kids study as thoroughly as Kim? Why is it that Julie and Danny never seem to disappoint? Why are so many of our best behaved and disciplined students also the most academically talented?

These are the young people we hope to graduate from public schools. Unfortunately, many leaders within education have somehow fooled themselves into believing that developing high academic standards (as though students like Andrew were merely reading comic books all day) and the associated assessments will result in the improvement of our students. Too many educational leaders have forgotten what makes great young adults great.

Years ago, a mother attending parent-teacher conferences was told that if every student was like her son, more people would choose a career in teaching. Her response was revealing. She looked at the well-intending teacher plainly and offered, "That was the idea."

THERE ARE VERY FEW ACCIDENTS

Despite the fact that humble parents and teachers are accustomed to deflecting praise for their skill with children, students like Andrew are not the result of pleasant accidents or minor miracles or even incredible luck. These impressive young people are also not a result of flashy academic standards, refined assessment strategies, and fierce accountability—unless, of course, these standards, assessments, and accountability stages are developed and owned by the very people working with the child to make him or her impressive. In short, great students are raised and educated by great adults.

Almost without exception, the most impressive young people share a common thread: there is at least one adult in the lives of these adolescents who assures the youngster that he or she was not yet a finished product. The best students are almost always the by-products of annoying adult interference.

Curriculum? Standards? Basic skills? These are necessary, of course, but these have also been emphasized to the point of draining an extraordinary amount of time, energy, and state educational money. The problem with emphasizing curriculum, assessment, and accountability is quite simple: the greatest academic standards on earth are tragically irrelevant without a great adult presence emphasizing successful habits.

How did Andrew become the student he was in high school? His mother was a wonderfully supportive yet tough woman, and his father was the high school assistant principal. We teachers would have needed an Olympic effort to screw up Andrew and his sisters.

Good grades, according to Andrew, were as assumed by his parents as the morning sunrise. Why? Because he was smart enough to earn good grades—end of discussion. The thought of misbehaving in school, whether it would consist of disrespecting a struggling teacher or student, starting a food fight in the cafeteria, or skipping class to smoke a cigarette in the parking lot, was unthinkable to the point of hilarious for Andrew.

"My dad would have killed me," he stated in an interview for this book. "The trouble I would have gotten from an angry teacher, an angry coach? That would have been nothing compared to what I would have gotten at home—nothing." And Andrew, like most model students, loves and cherishes his parents and is proud to sing their praises for raising him to be better than he could have been.

So where do educators enter the picture? After all, not all parents are high school assistant principals with great kid skills; many children will need great teachers far more than did Andrew Atchison. We cannot be naïve to the point of assuming everyone will suddenly begin to raise kids properly simply because researchers have identified some commonalities among successful young people and the effective adults in their lives, right? This is why we actually need standards, assessments, and accountability, right?

LITERATE SOCIETY?

Wrong. School districts need academic standards, assessments, and accountability for the same reasons districts needed them in the 1950s. The world is big and usually complicated, and not knowing how to read and write effectively will hinder one significantly. Basic math skills are essential in today's world, an understanding of scientific methodology could assist people with their thinking for a lifetime, a great high school civics and government course (or teacher) would easily teach young people more than one thousand televised presidential debates combined, and a working knowledge of current technology could be the difference between earning money and living in the parents' basement.

Of course school curriculum needs standards; it always has. But many educators have chosen to emphasize the wrong path in education. When the best students reflect on their education years after receiving it (an interesting concept), they do not reference curriculum. They do, however, remember that reporting to Mr. Hanson's class without completed homework was akin to backpacking across Africa without water.

"The guy was just a hard-ass, and somehow we all loved him." These were Andrew's words describing one of his high school teachers. He remembers very little about what was taught in this man's classroom, yet he has clarity about showing up on time, being respectful, and always having his assignments completed.

This is what the often-misled experts in education do not—or will not—acknowledge. Many young people at the university level boast an amazing high school GPA and ACT score. Even the most talented students do not remember Avogadro's number (chemistry), the rate of gravitational pull (physics), the rules of using a semicolon alone (grammar), and the capitol of Peru (world geography). They were tested on all of this material, and these are likely part of our nation's growing Common Core state standards (at least the English and math questions), but our best students do not remember the answers three years after graduating from high school.

America's best students, however, do remember the people who taught them to work, to be respectful, to develop perspective. They remember the adults who loved them by telling them uncomfortable truths when necessary and making them do difficult tasks when they mistakenly believed these tasks were impossible.

It is true: not enough parents do the job like Andrew's parents. It is also true that public educators are limited in the ways they can impact parenting (although not as limited as we pretend). We have no excuse, however, for underemphasizing the one key educational component from which nearly every successful high school graduate in this country has benefited: talented and responsible adults teaching effective, success-inducing, lifelong habits.

The most impressive and successful of young adults are not *literate* because of a district mandate to find the perfect books to read; they are *literate* because great adults made them read when they would have rather watched television.

HERE TO STAY?

Minnesota's Profile of Learning was repealed in 2003 and replaced with a shiny new alternative, the Minnesota Academic Standards. The new version centered on five core academic content standards: language arts, math, science, social studies, and the arts. Provided independent school districts could prove worthy, these districts were allowed to develop their arts standards locally.

More recently, the Graduation-Required Assessments for Diploma ("GRAD"—isn't that clever?) Program in Minnesota has aimed to better prepare students for college, highly skilled work, a civic life, or all of the above. The GRAD approach, however, hit a significant snag with its agenda. Specifically, far too many students were failing to accomplish the state math standard. The solution? These students were still able to graduate from high school, of course, provided they attempted at least two retests.

One of a few uncomfortable situations existed for a heavily funded educational standard policy to fall on its face this hard. First, no one in the state (or no one hoping to be reelected) was willing to keep *that many* high school seniors from graduating. Second, there appeared to be a significant number of highly skilled, responsible, even college-bound students struggling to pass the math standard.

This would lead to the conclusion that either the standard or the education the children of Minnesota received was flawed, right? Nope, it simply meant that passing the standard involves attempting the math test thrice—even if every effort results in failure.

Does anyone need to wonder how revered state and government academic standards are in the eyes of great parents and educators when the answer to a problem like significant math deficiencies is solved by simply asking students to retake the test until we thoroughly convince kids they are stupid?

Standards are likely here to stay, but Core Standards as we currently know them will be significantly altered or gone before most school districts can claim to have taken a child from kindergarten through twelfth grade. Yes, standards will remain—they will have a new, cool name and likely accomplish no more and no less than the program from the decade before—but they will remain.

Why will Core Standards inevitably fade away to make room for another idea? Because struggling schools and struggling students will still be struggling three, five, and ten years from now. Contrary to what those who choose to emphasize curriculum, assessment, and accountability claim, the answer to the agreed-upon educational issues will not be universally found via the creation of a great K–12 syllabus.

Will Common Core state standards be effective in some school districts across the country? Of course. These are the same schools that flourished with outcome-based education, No Child Left Behind, and the Profiles of Learning. These are also the same schools that have benefited from the wonderful mixture (and volume) of great parents and teachers raising and educating young people.

Test scores? These are merely a symptom of the overall education impressive adults deliver to their children. If concerned citizens want their school district to accomplish AYP, they would be wise to emphasize (demand), among other things, consistent attendance and diligent work in their district's schools. Of course faculty should be teaching language arts, math, science, social studies, and the arts. What else would they be doing?

How did Andrew Atchison become a great student without graduation standards? That is a trick question, and every good parent and teacher knows the right answer. He did have graduation standards; they were created by his impressive teachers and administrators and consistently reinforced by his parents at home. Andrew was raised and taught to be a successful member of a literate society, yet for the life of him he could not possibly remember today the answers to test questions he answered in the late 1990s.

Dr. Andrew Atchison is now a dentist in northern Minnesota. He loves his job, his growing family, and the life they are building. He plays golf whenever time allows. Like Andrew, his sisters are also enjoying productive, successful adult lives, and all of them maintain a significant and loving connection with their parents. Andrew insists he is no smarter than any of the people with whom he attended K–12 public school, yet he admits he has thrived. Why? "It's what I was raised to do."

Standards will remain. So, too, will disappointment with student test scores and the accomplishments of young people until we finally realize we are emphasizing all the wrong stuff.

FIVE

Teachers or Secretaries?

> "Your lesson plans should be so organized and thorough that any substitute could take your class for that period without a dip in quality." — Various K–12 administrators

The quote above is one of the dumbest utterances imaginable, yet generations of teachers have endured such words as they were delivered at staff meetings. A room full of forty-five to fifty teachers—and a principal assuring them that a teacher's presence in the classroom is only as relevant as the lesson plan. An inspirational message like this could only be rivaled by a district meeting detailing future budget cuts.

So, if the lesson plan is detailed enough, anyone could teach that fifth-period Grammar and Composition course with three autistic children, two foreign-exchange students, a boy on house arrest, a girl in a wheelchair, and a door spinning from steady special education assistance?

In defense of the droves of principals who have said something like this to their faculty (this ideology must have been standard fare for 1990s administration graduate schools), their intentions have likely been good. Teachers, after all, should be dedicated to producing organized, age-appropriate, highly engaging, and challenging lesson plans.

Further, when the regular classroom teacher is absent from school, it would be best if academia could march forward as a result of these impressive lesson plans to assist a substitute teacher—as opposed to offering seven periods of study hall resulting in spitball fights.

The quote about lesson plans and substitute teachers, however, hints at something far more significant than either potentially offending a room full of teachers or the importance of being organized. There is a tremendous misunderstanding, even among some leaders within the teaching profession, about what it is that great educators do.

If a substitute teacher can consistently equal or outperform the regular classroom teacher, creating user-friendly lesson plans is the least of concerns for both the regular instructor and the building principal. In the best public schools, the quality dips in the classroom any day a substitute teacher is present. Furthermore, with some thought, administrators can begin to understand why this reality is something to cherish not regret.

WHAT ALMOST ALL TEACHERS DO

Teachers obviously play a significant role in the delivery of academics. This is a truth nearly everyone in society can recognize; that is, what good is an English teacher if he is failing to effectively teach English curriculum to his students? The delivery of traditional curriculum capable of being assessed is paramount within a teacher's job description.

To begin, effective teachers must understand what it is they want their students to know or be able to do. Without these objectives, educators find themselves teaching anything and everything yet teaching nothing. What should students know at the end of the period? This question guides effective teachers, and any student accomplishments beyond these objectives are merely a result of good fortune.

"What are we doing today in class?" Every teacher has been asked this, and the answer is typically what separates the productive classrooms from the others. What teachers "do" is their action plan for accomplishing the objectives. When teachers effectively deliver curriculum via great lesson plans, students learn.

When lesson plans are ineffective, classrooms quickly become a school-based mirage, often appearing to be a fun and welcoming haven for students, but subsequently providing these children with little more than a room to mingle for fifty minutes or more. Worse yet, many ineffective lesson plans are accompanied by oppressive environments striking fear and resentment into students. Either way, objectives must lead to an appropriate plan of action—and one without the other produces chaos or worse.

Teachers who improve their performance do so not because they age, but because they are disciplined enough to assess and reflect upon both student learning and their own teaching. Is this what I want students to learn? Did the students learn? Is my method of teaching effective? What should I do better?

- Objectives
- Learning activities (the actual lesson plan)
- Assessment
- Reflection

These simple teaching staples are not to be undersold, for the skills are vital for successful schools. Children must learn to read and write, to show competence in math, to pass the state standard for science, and so on. This is what teachers do. Further, it is what the public, politicians, and educational leaders have come to expect from public educators.

Academic accomplishment via effective teaching has become public education's North Star. American educators, according to current ideology, are to produce students who test well. There is, however, an unfortunate reality associated with today's public education priorities. Stated simply, this emphasis is not working.

For starters, too many of our students are not testing well. With that, too many of our capable students who do test well are struggling for success after high school. Why? It is either because their skills fail to align within the parameters of the designated tests, or because we have not emphasized with these children what is required to be impressive.

As detailed in chapter 4, standards in Minnesota have been adapted to the point that students failing to pass the math portion of the state graduation requirement are nonetheless passed and eligible to graduate, provided they have attempted at least two retakes of the test.

How can this embarrassing problem exist? How did the experts in Minnesota not see this coming? It happens because sometimes really bright, capable young people struggle on tests (especially math). It also happens because educational experts are too often disconnected from reality as it relates to genuine success for children and young adults.

Educational experts at the state level are often befuddled by talented students underachieving on state-mandated tests. These seemingly capable kids do not test poorly because they are stupid or because the curriculum was not presented within their schools. In fact, the tested curriculum has likely become the primary focus for most classes these young people attend. These students fail to impress because they are the pawns of an educational philosophy that inexplicably emphasizes game days to the point where practice has become forgotten.

Ironically, it is the same reason so many young people, despite flourishing on these tests, struggle after high school graduation. College life, these students often learn, does not coincide with what has been emphasized in K–12 public education. It matters when college students fail to show up for class on a Tuesday morning. Work ethic, discipline, and timeliness, like many other defining habits, are learned. They are not, however, measurable Core Standards.

WHAT GREAT TEACHERS DO

Test scores are merely a symptom of an effective or ineffective education. Focusing efforts so that MAP testing, graduation standards, and the ACT are the finish line in public schools strips educators of their primary skill as it relates to working with children—teaching. Great teachers do focus on curriculum objectives and lesson plans, of course, yet the best deliver endlessly more than test scores. Teaching to the test? This is the work of educational secretaries. The substitute teacher can teach to the test.

What do great teachers do? They use curriculum, along with sports, music, clubs, student government, and everything else extra in school, as the horse to pull a wagon full of necessary life skills and habits.

Great math teachers, for example, likely have students with impressive test scores. How? Do these instructors have a really advanced text no other teachers could find? Did they just get lucky and have all the smart kids assigned to their schedule? We know better. Great math teachers are great because the bulk of their students would not dare walk into class late or without their homework completed.

The students in a great math teacher's class know better than to mess around when she is explaining polynomials. These kids know that at any moment they could be called upon to answer a question. They know that somehow, some way, this woman will likely use every last drop of the fifty minutes designated for third period. These students know that bathroom breaks are better spent well before or after class. The orthodontist appointment? No way, not during math class.

Cell phones? Falling asleep? Blurting out nonsense and thus distracting classmates? Making excuses for laziness? Blaming other people? Purposely disrespecting a peer or the instructor? Nope, not during math class. Great teachers have students who know better than to try that junk.

Yet, amazingly, this math teacher is also adored by her students. Her students come to her classroom before and after school for help, and sometimes they do not even need the assistance. Student council representatives ask her to chaperone nearly every dance. Even struggling students, those who consistently fail to make positive connections with adults, somehow tolerate her. Is she a nag? Yes, but she nags respectfully.

This great teacher also understands the significance of teaching complicated material to children and adolescents. She realizes that retention of her curriculum is tenuous at best, for years from now, when her students are adults, the rules of dividing fractions will likely be forgotten. This is fine, she knows, because although not all of her students will flourish in math as she has, very few of them will forget what it meant to thrive in her class. Kids do not forget those lessons; they apply them to other parts of their lives.

The substitute can be an educational secretary, not her. Hopefully, the academic material will be covered appropriately when this teacher is home with her sick child, but when she is in her classroom, polynomials are merely one piece of the puzzle that she and other great teachers like her strive to create with the kids they teach. This is what great teachers do.

TEACHER EVOLUTION

Teacher education courses rarely address the traits and habits emphasized by our best instructors; too few of the professors training our future teachers taught in the public schools long enough (or well enough) to understand the profession for what it really is. Neophyte teachers are prepared as well as possible in many cases, yet most within the teaching profession know that greatness is not something education professors can teach college students.

It is common for teachers to focus on themselves in the beginning of a career. Did I take attendance correctly? Did I teach everything I had planned? Did I look nervous? Am I ready for tomorrow? As experience is gained, they can further their academic delivery by focusing on the students. Do my students understand the five paragraph essay? Should I reteach the concept of leadoffs and follow-ups? How will my assessment of this homework affect the student?

Beginning teachers are thrown into the fire, and many leave for the safety and sanity of other professions before they complete three years in a classroom. Those who do survive are bombarded with the current curriculum standards and assessment information, and it becomes, by necessity, their guide. Many teachers and administrators never abandon the comfort zone of academic curriculum, assessment, and accountability. These are what many in education need—something visible, measurable, undeniable.

Great educators certainly do not neglect the vitality of traditional curriculum, assessment, and accountability; however, they eventually find themselves at a crossroads. Great teachers pay attention to both the process and the outcomes associated with teaching kids, and many begin to question what has been emphasized within their classrooms.

Why? Because it is actually not that difficult, at least for a great teacher, to teach a kid to write a five paragraph essay or balance an equation. The majority of students, great teachers find, are capable of learning most if not all of the curriculum offered. This fact does not satisfy the best teachers. If success is determined by merely displaying proficiencies within Common Core standards, success has been grossly mislabeled in schools.

What do my students need to be more impressive? What should I be doing about it? This is what genuine, effective educational leaders are asking while simultaneously delivering a rigorous academic curriculum. These questions, it seems, are the tough ones.

There are no high-quality veteran teachers in our society saying, "Wow, the basic principles of math and science sure have changed over these past thirty years!" No, the traditional curriculum does not evolve like students and their needs. Yet educators are being asked to focus on academics and assessment while young people are starving for a different educational emphasis.

One need only follow some of the most "successful" high school students beyond graduation to see this as truth. America's best students are often struggling in colleges, universities, and the workforce throughout this country. This fact is the discomforting secret our state- and national-level measure-mongers keep from public educators.

Failing to acknowledge the fact that today's young people badly need what no one is delivering—and that their needs often have nothing to do with academics—is irresponsible. Great teachers have known this for quite some time now, despite the fact that few if any of the state or national "experts" have bothered to truly examine the philosophy or tactics of these amazingly effective educators.

Our nation's teachers are being trained and paid to be educational secretaries. The best are nonetheless teaching.

SIX
The Unwritten Curriculum

This is certainly not the first book proclaiming the need for an unwritten curriculum. In fact, researchers have for years been calling for an emphasis in something beyond test scores. Thomas Lickona saw the need for character education in the early 1990s, and his work is more relevant today than it was even then.

In 1985, Neil Postman warned us about our children "amusing themselves to death" with technology and other creature comforts. Does anyone actually believe that the past thirty years have helped with this problem? Educators have made a healthy effort to use technology as a supplement, hoping to "hook" students into new-age learning. There is no question today's students are more capable than the kids of 1985 with technology, yet there is little evidence suggesting current students are in any way headed to the quality of life they plan on enjoying.

Endless studies exist about educational overhauls designed to somehow clean up messy American young people. Various school districts, typically urban, have turned to alternative emphases to counteract disappointing schools and communities. The new aim, often viewed as a drastic measure within these struggling districts, turned toward the teaching of respect, responsibility, trustworthiness, and work ethic—to name a few. Why? This is what was missing from the upbringing of too many children within these neighborhoods.

But what about the test scores? Were they not horribly substandard? Of course, but the teachers and administrators finally came to the realization that emphasizing tests was accomplishing nothing. Instead, these mavericks began to emphasize decent human behavior and success-inducing habits.

In many instances, these new approaches have worked. Where there are willing parents and great teachers and administrators, some schools have been reinvented to become a source of miracles for students in struggling communities. Drastic transformation of a school and a community's outlook toward education is rare, obviously, because it takes courage both to recognize weaknesses and to work to overcome them by going against the institutional grain.

Further, to almost everyone's surprise, some of these struggling schools also accomplish the unthinkable: test scores have improved. Many experts are tempted to associate inner-city success stories with whatever trendy "program" was used as a label. In reality, an educational program is not much more than a proper noun. Successful change within these settings has come from impressive adults who have both found a need and addressed it with full force.

The mistake made by the middle and upper-middle class, as well as those who both educate and represent them, is that they fail to recognize that middle-class children are struggling with the very same concepts holding back lower-income, inner-city youths: respect, responsibility, trustworthiness, and work ethic—to name a few. Why? This is what is missing from the upbringing of too many children within middle-class neighborhoods.

But rich white kids from the suburbs cannot be suffering from the same symptoms afflicting inner-city youths, can they? These are the young people attending our nation's universities, the children of the best and brightest, right? There are several responses for questions like these, and few of them are reassuring for those outside of the educational loop. The status of America's best and brightest is not what many mistakenly presume.

What was once a concern for only the most disadvantaged students is now a reality for a generation of American children. The middle-class kids in this country—along with their parents and many educators—are the frogs slowly losing their capabilities in a soon-to-be-boiling pan of water.

GREAT ADULTS

Chapter 4 of this book describes Andrew, a 1990s high school student from Minnesota. He graduated before implementation of the state's Profile of Learning (an aggressive standards-based overhaul of public education), yet he was a model student by the standard of any public school.

Andrew thrived in the classroom, excelled in athletics and the arts, and proved to be a leader among his peers. It is important to note, however, that Andrew was not extraordinary to the point of having no explanations or reference points. He was not Einstein, Beethoven, or Tiger Woods; he was an average kid with a good intellect.

He had good pals, he made mistakes, he ate hot lunch, he chased girls, he listened to terrible music, and he was a perfect fit for the high school culture awaiting him. Everything about him was average—except for the fact that he was raised to be above average. Andrew was not armed with magic from the gods of school excellence, he was armed with great parents and a crew of good teachers.

Andrew's description furthers a point. If all classrooms were filled with students like him, and if all communities were full of parents like his, the United States would have much different concerns in public education than it currently has. Imagine the opportunities for schools if the public more resembled Andrew's parents and insisted that their children perform to their abilities while maintaining a sense of decency.

Imagine the capabilities of high school and college graduates under these circumstances. The progress the nation's teachers could make while teaching the children of great adults would be staggering. America's system of public education would have no peers; it would redefine concepts like AYP to reflect a wealth of youth accomplishment no country on earth could even hope to rival.

Imagine society itself. With a citizenry full of amazing people, most could actually differentiate between two political candidates and vote without needing either Fox News or MSNBC to tell them what to think. The capabilities of United States citizens would obliterate what is currently perceive as the middle class if the bulk of kids attended school with the adult presence they deserve.

But this is not reality as it relates to education in the United States. Public school classrooms are sorely lacking the great students older citizens seem to remember as being more common on the class lists of yesteryear. The results? There are gloomy test scores, ill-prepared college students, and a dark underbelly many in education wish they could not see: a generation of unimpressive, unproductive, often-misguided, and morally deficient young adults. And this is merely the picture seen in schools.

The community experiences the problem of unimpressive young adults immediately after these kids graduate from high school. Whether the issue centers on the talented yet lazy college student or the young man or woman expecting a pay raise and two weeks' vacation the day after starting at McDonald's, the working society is growing tired of the trend.

Entitlement is merely one of the unpleasant characteristics being displayed by the nation's freshly graduated. Hundreds of articles and books have been written about the "state" of young adults, and these researchers provide an endless list of reasons for this discouraging news.

The prevailing reaction to this problem, at least within public K–12 education, has been clearly stated within the opening chapters of this book. Educational leaders have injected traditional K–12 curriculum

(English, math, science) with steroids. We have decided exactly what it is we want our kids to know, and we test the snot out of them to make certain they know it.

Great adults, specifically parents and teachers, are responsible for the transformation of children and adolescents into impressive, productive, and good adults. Curriculum standards and appropriate assessments are a noble pursuit, yet believing great young people will result from this emphasis alone is sadly naïve. Further, overemphasizing these tactics has stripped the value of educators. Teachers teach. Facilitators? Test coordinators? Teaching to the test? This is the work of secretaries.

Who are the best teachers? Those with an amazing grasp of their subjects? Perhaps, but anyone who has studied Hemingway knows he would not have been a great fit for an eighth-grade English classroom, nor do many of the NASA scientists likely have the "kid skills" to survive twenty-five sophomores itching to use the Bunsen burners. The best adults—the award-winning educators and the wisest of parents—also teach the unwritten curriculum.

CARING OUR KIDS TO FAILURE?

It is difficult to describe great adults, however. One of the most common causes of young-adult failure is rooted in the fact that, more often than not, the adults who have been responsible for these kids have, ironically, cared a great deal about them. Caring, moreover, does not necessarily equate to quality when it involves effectively parenting and educating young people.

Many in education have been lulled into agreeing that, because people "care" a great deal about something associated with kids or schools, it must be acceptable and worthwhile and educationally sound. This is flawed thinking.

It is unacceptable for leaders in education to dote on the every want and need of students, parents, teachers, and even coaches as it relates to their happiness. Not every gripe registered by Mr. and Mrs. Jones requires the school administration to assemble for the purpose of placation.

Not every accomplishment involving athletics requires a pep rally. Not every teacher should be fine with students consistently leaving school early in the spring to decorate for prom. There are countless examples making the point that inappropriate, obsessive passion for anything related to education is worse than no passion at all.

Great adults care about children without thinking like children. They are not to be burdened with the worry about what our kids want right here, right now. They do not rearrange their lives to provide every last drop of what children want.

Why? Because the best adults know that approach to parenting and educating creates the proverbial fat, dumb, and temporarily happy youngster. Instead, responsible adults are called to teach children how to succeed in life by emphasizing the habits that may not come naturally in the moment.

Sports, for example, are a source of passion for millions of our nation's children and adolescents. The vast majority of these young athletes have no need for additional sport-related "care" from the adults in their lives—they have teammates, coaches, and an abundant supply of youthfulness to keep their passion for sport burning hot.

What do many of these kids want? They are kids; what they want is for their passions to be endlessly provided for and supported without fail. We see this in America when family mealtime has become subservient to the weight-lifting schedule, when the fifteen-year-old kid and his choice of sport dictates the type of vehicle mom and dad must drive (hockey equipment takes up space), and when grown men and women refinance their homes so their children can attend the out-of-state camps promising to improve their performance on the court next season.

What most children need, however, is a different story. Great adults provide opportunities for their children, obviously, but kids do not run the show in the home of great adults. Want to play sports, child? Fantastic. Want me to call the coach whenever you are upset? Dream on. The best adults care about their children enough to disappoint them in the short term again and again.

While others are worried about the upcoming playoffs or stressed about the plays called in the game last week or even clamoring for the coach's head on a spear, great adults are teaching their children how to handle the successes and failures associated with life's passions. With that, they are steadfastly demanding of their children that sports remain one piece of the school puzzle—not the puzzle itself.

Sports are merely one sample of how adults often care about their children ineffectively. Traditional academic curriculum and extracurricular activities come together to define much of what educational leaders hope to provide for the nation's youth. Furthermore, how adults deliver these opportunities, and what they teach while providing these, will determine how successful young people can become.

Great teachers bundle both their traditional curriculum and the extracurricular activities into a blanket of successful habits and life skills, and they wrap students in it every day. They know that most of what they test will be forgotten within weeks if not days after the exam. They know that no one at a high school reunion remembers numbers on a scoreboard. This unwritten curriculum, ironically, is what students remember—and use—years after answers to important tests have been forgotten. This is how impressive parents and teachers "care" children to success.

THE UNWRITTEN CURRICULUM

Effective parents and educators throughout the country could likely add to the list of unwritten curriculum essentials outlined in this book. After all, much of what great adults teach is formulated from what children need—and, in many cases, knowing what youths need is impossible until an effective relationship has been established.

That admitted, there are habits children need to learn from responsible, wise, and willing adults. Furthermore, whether these kids are fortunate enough to have fantastic role models in the home, or if their positive adult influences are limited to what can be offered in the schools, the job as an impressive adult, whomever he or she may be, is to establish—and emphasize—a culture of successful behavior and habits.

Part 3 of this book, "Great Habits of the Unwritten Curriculum," details the following points of emphasis:

- Children and young adults learning must learn *age-appropriate thinking skills* (chapter 7). Teachers and parents are hurting young people by allowing them to believe that "smart" is the ability to remember something. Students will forget curriculum, yet they will benefit from an ability to critically think for the remainder of their lives. This is one of the secrets nearly all successful adults know, and we are irresponsible without the courage to teach it.
- The teaching of *age-appropriate people and communication skills* (chapter 8) is necessary to protect young men and women from being completely disregarded. Intelligence? High test scores? Outside of a select few career options, these are irrelevant without the ability to demonstrate people skills and communicate effectively.
- What does "on time" mean for successful people? *Timeliness and attendance* (chapter 9) must be taught, it seems, because there exists a generation of young people who have been raised to believe that the party starts when they arrive—and not a minute before. The difference between casual time and professional time is sometimes nonexistent within public schools, and this reality is hurting young people in college, the workforce, and beyond.
- *Work ethic and dedication* (chapter 10) have no peers within the unwritten curriculum. Youths absolutely must understand what it means to "follow through" before they can claim a success. Work ethic not only leads to academic growth, but it is also responsible for overcoming academic struggles. Great parents and educators consistently teach the value of hard work. School should be challenging for all students. If it is not, we are not preparing our students for success.
- Teaching *respect, decency, and humility* (chapter 11), unfortunately, has too often become the responsibility of public educators. Boast-

ing about AYP, average ACT scores, or a school's sports accomplishments is shameful if accompanied with students' failure to treat others well. Great adults associated with public schools need only to ask two questions regarding respect and decency: What do we expect from our students? What will we not tolerate?
- In good schools, what happens when a teacher sees a student miss the garbage can with a tossed wad of trash only to keep strolling along his merry way? Who picks it up? There are countless steps adults can take to emphasize the habits of *responsibility and teamwork* (chapter 12). If the habits are reinforced, children will learn the value of carrying their own water (without praise) whenever possible and the buckets of others (without praise) when necessary.
- The most successful of adults are capable of seeing a bigger picture. *Perspective* (chapter 13) is one of the greatest gifts we can give a high school graduate; there is an endless value in learning that we know next to nothing—as long as we embrace this reality as a challenge. Whether we teach perspective via a great classroom discussion, with a thought-provoking assignment, or by enduring an embarrassing loss on the basketball court, this is the lesson, above all others, that requires a strong, wise adult.

EVERYONE'S PROBLEM

Children become what influential adults emphasize. This is great news, provided adults prove themselves capable of recognizing what it is kids need. The "Great Habits of the Unwritten Curriculum" briefly introduced in this chapter are no longer a safe assumption; students do not arrive at school hardwired with these necessary traits. Ironically, some of our nation's most challenged, economically stressed school districts arrived at this conclusion well before everyone else. The noble educators working with these disadvantaged youths recognized the insanity of continuing to emphasize something that does not stand a chance of producing favorable results.

How long will it take the rest of us to come to this conclusion? There is little doubt that if our nation's best parents and educational leaders could follow the so-called best students into the college setting, there would be a quick reassessment of what it is we are emphasizing in public schools.

Why? Our most talented students are struggling mightily at almost everything we claim to be emphasizing in K–12 schools. American education problems are no longer exclusive to poverty-stricken families within our inner cities; the need for an unwritten curriculum has entered every zip code.

Part Three

Great Habits of the Unwritten Curriculum

SEVEN
Age-Appropriate Thinking Skills

TEACHING TO THE TEST

This is not the first publication bemoaning the current state of affairs in public education as it relates to the overemphasis of testing. In fact, the majority of adults connected to the actual teaching of children in school are opposed to the amount of tests students are enduring. Every day used to test, to measure our young people, great educators know, is a day taken away from teaching them.

These tests have become the goal of school district leaders, however, because no one in public education is encouraged to argue with the results they reflect. It is in this vein that public education in America has become a business of knowing facts. Why? Facts are measurable; the measure-mongers can test for these. Furthermore, student retention of facts has become the ultimate comparison between "adequate" schools and those needing improvement.

North High is a better school than South High—the parents care more, the administrators are better, the teachers are superior, the PLCs are more productive, the kids are smarter, and the future is brighter. We know this because we have test scores to back it up.

Few follow the North High students to college and notice that they actually have no significant abilities beyond the South High students attending the same college. Can they read and write fluently (no small task)? Do they have functional math skills? After these (admittedly, Core Standards have value), very little a young person memorized in school will be relevant at the next level.

Clearly, facts are essential for student success. Even the most abstract among us cannot deny the necessity for students to know the alphabet, the multiplication tables, and the basic differences between the executive and legislative branches of the United States government. Facts are important; they are the necessary building blocks of a great American public education. This, however, has nothing to do with why the measure-mongers are infatuated with facts in public schools.

Facts fit on the scale, and many educational experts are losing interest with spending any time whatsoever on academics that cannot be measured. This may not bother those outside of K–12 education, but it should. Teaching to the test in American schools is failing on several fronts. To begin, despite the best of efforts, struggling students still cannot seem to remember all the facts they are asked to remember.

Current public education ideology approaches disenfranchised students with an unbearably shallow educational philosophy. Why are the students at South High struggling? What can fix these poor kids? Success, as it is sold, will be within their grasp as soon as teachers and administrators can figure out a way to have them pass some tests. The prevailing strategy with traditionally poor performers is basically the equivalent of asking them to memorize phone numbers instead of learning how to use a phone book when necessary.

Instinctively, great teachers know better. Students are not struggling because they have not learned the answers; they have not learned the answers because they are struggling. The best teachers break down the barriers of disenfranchised students by building a relationship with these children and teaching them, among other things, to think critically about themselves and the world around them.

In many cases, these great educators are the only people in the world who have taught these young people how to think. Test scores? If they do improve, it is only as a by-product of learning how to be successful in school and beyond.

The same could be found with the best and brightest students. They make parents and teachers proud by remembering several phone numbers. Moreover, educators somehow convince themselves that their test scores actually reflect the great education delivered. In reality, even the most successful students, those who prove capable of reciting every list given to them, too often flounder after high school graduation.

The capital of Argentina? Avogadro's number? Every middle school student in the United States has been asked about the capital of Argentina. Every decent high school science class has addressed Avogadro's number. Yet strikingly few readers of this book can identify either answer without doing research. Does this make us stupid?

Despite the fact that teachers tested for accuracy and these answers were likely known on test day, such facts are forgotten before Thanksgiving of the freshman year of college. This does not expose the best students as dullards; it merely sheds light upon a reality of teaching to the test.

Teaching to the test has left much of public school curriculum tasteless, narrow, and argument-free. Although it cannot be debated that having an impressive command of information is beneficial for young people, children need more than what is currently being emphasizing. Schools are playing a significant role in producing a generation of young people underprepared to either ask or answer the questions "Why?" and "What if?"

Whereas public schools have been emphasizing adequate producers (human copy machines rewarded for impressive memory and answer reproduction), the truly successful have learned to raise questions, to struggle with the unknown, to form a researched opinion—to think. State and national tests do very little to measure thinking. Worse yet, because of these tests, many teachers are doing very little to teach thinking.

THE LIE WE TELL OURSELVES

Learning—significant, impressive learning—is not easy. It requires copious work from both those who are teaching and, subsequently, the students attempting to learn. In many ways, educators have forgotten this. Certainly, teachers are aware that it is challenging to have students know what educators want them to know (ask any public school teacher/administrator struggling with students to accomplish AYP). Attaining 100 percent proficiency in reading and math scores is nothing short of a fairy tale for most public school districts.

Public schools educate everyone aside from those enrolled within home, private, or charter schools and the incredibly small percentage of children who cannot be in school. AYP scores? Critics of public schools too easily forget that public school teachers are called to instruct immigrants and refugees for whom English is a second or third language.

Few understand that countless children come from homes where parents have never read to them. Assessment experts conveniently avoid the list of setbacks facing millions of children in public schools. It is worthy to note, moreover, that the vast majority of these unfortunate children take the tests used to measure adequate educational progress.

The assessments developed for the measuring of public education are incredibly revealing, yet the experts are having some trouble seeing the forest for the trees. Although the data sometimes suggests it, struggling children are not dumb and their teachers are only as ineffective as their requirements to "teach to the test." Students are performing in school exactly how they should be expected to perform—and this, it must be noted, is the root of the lie educational experts keep telling themselves.

America's fortunate students, often the best and brightest, make a mockery of AYP. These young people are sent to kindergarten knowing their alphabet and some simple math, they are well-fed, they are consistently put to bed on time, they feel safe, their parents help them with homework, and their test scores have been reflecting it. Mediocre teachers can lead these students to AYP; furthermore, the most fortunate students pass standards without being significantly challenged. This is troublesome.

The truly unfortunate students, although often no less intelligent than their peers, are fighting an uphill battle in schools from the instant they walk into their first classroom. Because success has been labeled and the assessment process is guiding educational practice, public school teachers are charged with preparing these struggling students to somehow, some way pass the tests.

School success in this country has been established as what one knows by the time he or she reaches a certain grade. The most unfortunate of students can be taught by the best of teachers, they can be challenged greatly while intellectually growing, they can have their lives changed for the better because of school, and even then they may not make AYP. This too is troublesome.

TEACHING STUDENTS TO THINK

Successful young people like Andrew (described earlier in this book) have been taught to think. It takes courage for educators to require critical thinking—that which cannot fit into a rubric—from students. Ironically, courage is one of the amazing by-products attained by students as they are taught to question, to reflect, to struggle, to adapt—to think.

Imagine the strength of character required for our most impressive adolescent students to break free from ignorance and significantly change. When a sixteen-year-old white boy realizes that, as opposed to what he has believed in the past, Hispanic people are not worthless, it takes courage. He now has a Hispanic teammate on the football team, and that boy is no different than any of his other friends. He decides there is no reason he should avoid sitting next to this Hispanic boy at lunch; furthermore, he concludes that anyone who has a problem with it is ignorant.

Little realities like this happen in schools every day in America. Young people are changed; they are improved by an environment that constantly begs more of them than what they had the day before. The sixteen-year-old white boy who was being slowed by racist ignorance was given the best education America can offer. He had several great teachers and a coach or two who put him in an environment that challenged his flawed ideologies. Despite the fact that it was never referenced on a syllabus and never assessed with a number two pencil, this boy was taught to think.

Inexplicably, educators too often fail to teach critical thinking during the actual class periods. This is when and where teachers fear the mess that critical thinking creates. Instead, it is easier to distribute clean information and periodically check to see if students can reproduce it for a grade.

How is it possible to teach high school English without having a debate, an argument, or even a conversation about what an author is trying to accomplish with a piece of literature? How can anyone even dream of teaching a history course without seriously reflecting on the positives and negatives of our past and how these relate to our present?

Great K–12 educators recognize the need to teach critical thinking, and they will forge ahead with it, sometimes at the price of scorn from their colleagues. Learning to think critically is messy; sometimes kids say stupid things and their teachers are charged with reteaching the art of such thought. The mess makes it easy for teachers to choose the method of distributing clean information and periodically checking to see if students can reproduce it for a grade. Students can earn impressive grade point averages and class rankings via this methodology, yet they are often exposed at the next level for what they cannot do.

The best college students define themselves not by marching in an academic line, checking off their rubrics to assure themselves of an A. They are organized, of course, and with that trait comes an ability to complete work on time and in a form deemed acceptable by their professors. This should be expected of college students, however. The successful students in higher education are separated from their peers because they are capable of participating with the curriculum beyond a simple completion of assignments and assessments.

Top-tier college students can read a text and talk about it the next day in class without requiring three small-group members to interpret for them. They are not afraid to have an opinion about course content and do not struggle connecting the studied material to their own experiences when necessary.

These students view major paper rubric requirements as guidelines if not limitations, not a blueprint for an A. They sometimes disagree with what is presented in class, yet they are capable of recognizing their own flawed reasoning when it is presented to them. These students are, in essence, thinkers.

How can public educators generate more top-tier college students? Teachers can start by squashing the incessant need for all assignments to have a rubric, the "blueprint for an A." This nonsense is killing the most capable students, and most below-average to average students are using rubrics to do little more than exactly what they are told to do. College and university professors are inundated with masses of twenty-year-old men and women who steadfastly require their instructors to tell them what to do.

Rubrics do have a place in schools, but educators should be careful about associating them too closely with an actual *education*. A well-constructed rubric, rather, is a perfect guideline to *train* someone. "Stop, drop, and roll," one of the most effective rubrics created, is a great training tool to teach people what to do in the event of starting on fire. Why? If anyone has a question about the interpretation of "stop, drop, and roll," he probably should not have access to anything flammable.

Rubrics should be used when critical thinking is unnecessary. In fact, they are best used when critical thinking could be dangerous—"stop, drop, and roll," for instance. Writing a paper about the Cold War and its influences on the economies of Western civilization? Aside from number of pages desired and a few APA or MLA guidelines, a detailed, color-by-number rubric has no business interfering with this assignment.

Students deserve the opportunity to create a product (a paper, for example) and receive critical feedback about subjective assignments. But what if the kid struggles? What if the assignment is completely awful? This is the opportunity to teach students something they will not forget. This is the moment that separates educators from secretaries; anyone can give a kid a checklist and hold her hand while she completes a foolproof task. But effective teachers do not give assignments their students are incapable of completing.

Educators owe it to youths to ask more questions without undeniable answers. It is amazing what can happen in a young person's mind when one of three questions are asked of her with an expectation that thought is required.

- Why?
- Why not?
- What if?

Why did the United States wait so long to enter World War II? Why does our local government resist making recycling mandatory? What if Shakespeare actually did not write the plays for which he is credited? Why is there no need for a comma in this sentence? What would happen if high school student athletes were allowed to consume alcohol and use tobacco products? These questions require thoughtful insight, and this is a learned habit.

Once it becomes a habit, young people become further capable of thinking critically. What if I use this credit card to go on vacation? Why do I receive praise at work? Why was my coworker fired? What if I worked all summer to pay for half of my tuition? What if I used my money to get a tattoo instead of car insurance? Why can Grandpa afford a lake home?

Are we teaching young people how to think, or are we assuming it is happening somewhere else? The fact is it is often not happening somewhere else. Too many children are not being raised and educated to think. They are being raised and educated either to do and know what they are told (not always a good thing) or to do whatever feels good (even worse). These children are no different than many successful adults were years ago, with one exception: the parents and teachers of those adults refused to tolerate thinking beneath their capabilities.

Thinking is a great habit. It is taught.

EIGHT
Age-Appropriate People and Communication Skills

COMFORT AND CONVENIENCE RULE THE DAY

Young adults wear pajamas (or worse) in public, and almost no one is willing to tell them they look too ridiculous to be taken seriously. This may be due to the fact that it has become the norm for forty-year-old men and women to present themselves as though they are battling the stomach flu while shopping for groceries, traveling in an airplane, or even attending parent-teacher conferences.

Despite the fact that taboos against such habits as presenting one's self as a slob are vanishing in society, there remains a cutting reality about how we present ourselves and our chances for success: if we look and sound like children, we will be treated like children.

This book emphasizes several habits young people must learn, and few are as brutally straightforward as the necessity to impress (or at least avoid depressing) others with what they see and hear from us. Appropriately presenting ourselves and communicating with purpose is essential for long-term success; furthermore, these abilities are not attained by good fortune.

Young people *learn* how to handle themselves in a world full of non-relative others; they are *taught* these skills from the adults who know enough to model. Some youths are blessed with parents or other relatives capable of teaching them age-appropriate people and communication skills; unfortunately, school is the only place in the world many children will have access to impressive, well-spoken, appropriately dressed adults.

Chapter 8

THE MESSAGE SENT IS NOT ALWAYS THE MESSAGE RECEIVED

Not long ago, an undergraduate student stopped by his professor's office to ask about a grade he earned on a paper. From beginning to end, the conversation was one bad turn after another for this young man. With intentions of improving the score on an assignment, he instead revealed himself as one badly needing a different form of guidance.

"Uh, hey. You got a minute?" The professor was facing the other direction as the young man grunted this question. The teacher subsequently turned from his desk to see in the doorway this twenty-one-year-old man looking like someone paid him to intentionally look as horrible as possible. He was wearing sweatpants and a tank top made by cutting the sleeves off a T-shirt and around the collar; this choice of shirt left much of his torso exposed. As his tattered sweats were drooping, four to five inches of his boxer shorts were visible. To top off this ensemble, he wore a giant flat-brimmed baseball hat, presumably to cover his bed-head and morning eye gunk.

It is important to remember that the student initiated this meeting, not the other way around. He intentionally left his apartment to find his teacher in his office because he had an issue important enough for a face-to-face discussion. He planned this meeting, and it would have been nearly impossible for him to present himself any worse.

"Do you mean Dr. Tufte?" Few professors enjoy being snooty about their title, and many have friends who refer to them with an extreme sense of informality. "Uh, hey" is what a friend says after his buddy forgets his debit card on the counter at McDonald's; educators and students must protect themselves from casual, informal relationships with the foresight that even the best and brightest students may need guidance that a pal cannot offer.

After discussing the proper (and polite) way to address a professor, the teacher asked the young man to shut the door and sit down. They spoke about his choice of wardrobe, the incredible informality with which he spoke, that his face looked like he was merely minutes out of his bed, and the fact that all of this was actually planned.

The student was studying to become a secondary teacher. Really? This presentation of self, the professor explained, was professionally damning. This is what we wear to the emergency room in the middle of the night. This is how we talk to the best of our friends when there is no need for polish. But he and his teacher did not have a relationship for such informality; moreover, he will likely never be close enough with most of his future students, colleagues, or administrators to overcome this type of impression.

If there is a time and a place to look like a slob, in a professor's office when you need a favor is most definitely not it. This student was assured that he (along with every other student) is being judged every day and in every class. In today's world, telling a young person something like this is akin to offending his race or religion. Nonetheless, young people deserve the cold truth from responsible adults.

What do people think of you when you have your underwear exposed? What does your professor think when you are using your cell phone while she is lecturing? Are we old folks being judgmental? Of course we are. Can our students choose to ignore us? Of course. Poor grades, being refused for a letter of recommendation, and unemployment, however, are far more uncomfortable than being mildly offended from time to time.

Granted, this was not the chat the student had in mind that morning. An education professor's job, however, is to prepare undergraduate students to be effective teachers. If the teacher would have simply spoken with him about the paper and let him go about his merry way, he would have been lying to him. Amazingly, conversations like these are not at all uncommon for college instructors.

This young man is not an isolated example; he is merely one of a generation of genuinely nice, reasonably intelligent, capable youths who have yet to learn that the world is not their basement. This student had no idea he was sending the messages he was; to this point in his life, he had never learned to consider the relevance of his appearance and speaking ability.

The problem is not simply that young people come to classes in ratty sweatpants and belt-free, five-sizes-too-big jeans (underwear exposed, of course), and stylish hats and unable to focus their eyes without exposing the eye gunk they have yet to remove from their afternoon nap. These characteristics are unsightly, obviously, but the damage is done not by the wardrobe itself—but by the demeanor created by consistently dressing and acting like a slob hanging out in your parents' basement. The willingness to keep young people comfortable whenever and however they want is creating people who look ridiculous in times of importance. Countless parents and schools condone this. Stated more appropriately, countless parents and schools teach this.

Scores of America's high schools appease the need of students to express themselves. Consequently, students have taken comfort to new levels. Boys and girls alike will cruise the halls of academia in slippers and pajamas, often finding the class sofa for some quality snuggle time during the lesson. They wear hats whenever they want because, well, it does not seem to hurt anything.

If it feels good and it does not seem to cause trouble, it must be okay. In an effort to respect and appease adolescent students, secondary teachers and administrators have often lost the necessary edge required of a day in school. After all, when the kids are happy, they are easier to manage.

Educators allowing their schools to look like this are not managing their students; their students are managing them. Comfort, comfort, comfort . . . nonsense. The twenty-one-year-old who visited his professor looking like a homeless person was set back five years because of prioritizing comfort.

What he needed in high school was a group of caring, passionate teachers who provided discomfort when assignments were late, who did not drool over him because he was a skilled athlete, and who demanded he sit up straight, take off his hat, wear a belt, and speak to his capabilities. He deserved to be respected by the adults in his life.

DOWNLOADING SUCCESS

From educational leadership to juried academic journals to countless tweets regarding potential Core Standard amendments, technology literacy is the rage. Technology, as current ideology dictates, is the great equalizer—education's magic bullet. Desperate and lost are the young people without access to lightning-fast computers.

Leaders in education lament the impossibility for some school districts of allocating adequate funding for technology. Few, including this author, disagree with the necessity of educating youths to use cutting-edge technology. The benefits are endless and undeniable, right? Tech-savvy young people are primed for success, right?

But what do tech-savvy graduates look like? They are no different than student athletes, musicians, or any other graduate. Some are truly impressive while others underwhelm. Why? Content knowledge only goes so far. Today's young people must be taught how to communicate effectively, to impressively handle themselves with people, especially adults. Far too many otherwise talented youths do not appropriately interact with anyone outside of their closest friends or family. Thus far, technology does little to improve these necessary skills.

Additionally, many within public schools have forgotten what makes technology so wonderful: it is easy. An eighteen-year-old can likely learn a tech-related skill in fifteen minutes or less. Even adults experience this; countless are the schools requiring some students to teach a forty-five-year-old teacher how to turn something on and have it run properly. Laptops, cell phones, and iPods are better understood by children; it cannot be denied.

In today's world, technology literacy basically amounts to having access to it. It is not uncommon to hear stories of economically challenged school districts receiving a grant or other donations to use for technology. It is astonishing to witness how quickly a kid can become a whiz with a computer. Like many things, a little time to practice and play can teach a child more than anyone could ever dream. Computers give great feedback to kids and adults alike; when we make mistakes the computer redirects us. We adjust, and things work.

No one ever finalizes a grant to teach people skills, however. Overcoming the absence of appropriate people and communication skills can prove daunting if not impossible for young adults who cannot manage to look an adult in the eyes while offering a dead-fish handshake.

Can you create a SMART Board presentation? Who cares! That can be learned in the time it takes to mow my lawn. Can you survive giving this presentation if and when the SMART Board fails? This is a skill separating successful graduates from the others.

Parents and educators hope graduates are strong readers, writers, and mathematicians. These skills are essential, obviously, and so too is the ability to function in a technical society. Talented young people reflect the emphasis placed on these academics. It does not go unnoticed, however, that a great percentage of the best and brightest (and, subsequently, all the others) are actually acting like computers. This is hurting them when life calls for an ability to understand and affect humanity.

HUMAN INTERACTION

It is troubling to imagine struggling young adults—like the young man described in this chapter—conducting themselves in situations requiring adult people and communication skills. Educators clearly understand the necessity of knowing basic grammar and at least a minimal application of math ability. Adults too often neglect an obligation they have to prepare children for life beyond the test.

Students are, in many instances, merely weeks or months away from negotiating a salary or asking for a pay raise. How well will this work for the young man or woman who has not been taught to maintain eye contact during a conversation? "Um, hey.... Um, I was ... like wondering ... um ... could I, like ... get more money?" Responsible parents and teachers know better than to allow this to emit from young people.

Young adults will be called upon to defend a decision in the not-too-distant future; perhaps they will even feel a need to apologize for something. These conversations are often uncomfortable for even the most polished of professionals, for they require the confidence to present one's self well in a private, face-to-face setting that provides no reset button.

Steve manages a small group of young men in their midtwenties to early thirties at a company offering computer support and data security for businesses. A few months ago, three of these men stormed into their boss's office (Steve) and demanded a "conversation." It seems they were, collectively, feeling quite underpaid.

So the ranting and raving (with a healthy dosage of vulgarity) began. The unified men talked about how they have been working for this company long enough to deserve more money, how they could easily take a job "down the road" for more money, how unfair they believe they have been treated, and how they will simply quit if they do not get what they want. Their boss, silently listening and taking notes, waited for the trio to conclude their collective-bargaining tactics before he spoke. When he did speak, the young men received a reaction they did not predict.

"Well, I think the first thing I need to do is get some ads going for three new openings here." Shocked, the threesome looked for answers.

"You're firing us?"

"No, you just told me you have other jobs lined up with people willing to pay you more money than you make here. What choice do I have?"

It was at this point the actual conversation began. The unfortunate young men were quickly exposed; their inability to think like grown men led them to embarrassment. Their inability to communicate like grown men, however, nearly cost them their jobs.

What these men did not realize is damning to their bank accounts. If any one of them would have had the capability to actually schedule a meeting with Steve and have a conversation about his concerns (instead of planning a group attack and using empty threats), there is a decent chance his needs would have been met. There is no doubt whatsoever that things would have turned out better.

A story like this can be immediately traced back to education. This pathetic display of communication skills was, at worst, learned. At best, it is the result of never learning (and never being taught) how to work with people. Sadly, this is not uncommon behavior for young adults.

If impressive adults do not teach children to effectively communicate, they run the risk of developing long-lasting embarrassing habits. This should be a priority in homes and within public classrooms; adults must acknowledge its importance within all the subtle pieces they have in play for youths.

Is there a problem with the volleyball coach? Students are ultimately hurt when mom and dad are allowed to conduct this business without the student athlete required to represent herself and her own point of view. Want more playing time? Any solution that does not involve the student athlete and the coach is teaching the young person the wrong lesson.

If mom and dad can attain their daughter's playing time by going to the activities director—or a school board member—the student learns that direct communication with someone is not necessary as long as there is a way to go above his or her head (with assistance, of course).

Great parents and teachers emphasize age-appropriate people and communication skills at every turn. They are often a nuisance to their students. "Try asking that question again, John. This time, look up at me and don't mumble." This was a third-grade teacher from thirty years ago. She was adored.

"My God, we're not in our secret tree fort; shake my hand like a man!" This was a high school basketball coach. This author will never forget that one-sided conversation with him about how men shake hands.

"Are you, like, going to the mall to, like, buy some, like, clothes and stuff?" This one of countless high school English teachers reinforcing the need for us to raise the bar when we deliver public speeches. "It matters," she will say, "because we spend most of our lives talking to people who do not know or care about our inside jokes."

We perhaps do not have standardized tests for eye contact or shaking a hand or speaking without mumbling or even making sense while offering an opinion. Nonetheless, we are failing our children if we do not teach these habits. The world, it seems, is testing for these skills every day.

NINE
Timeliness and Attendance

WHAT WOULD GRANDPA THINK?

The college students of yesteryear—say, from the 1960s and '70s—would likely be shocked with what they would see in university classrooms of today. Online courses? The presentation abilities made possible by educational software? How bad PowerPoint presentations have become? Clearly, the capabilities related to technology would make an impression on many of our students from the past, but this alone would not leave anyone struck with awe. Technological updates are not confined to schools, after all.

The grandparents of today's students would be rendered speechless if they witnessed the casual nature displayed by young people toward showing up for work (or a class) and seeing it through. They would likely ignore everything else happening in a modern university classroom and focus instead on the revolving door of tardy students, students leaving early for orthodontist appointments, and the empty chairs from students who never arrived. Further, they would marvel at how the professors often embrace this approach by students and even display it themselves from time to time.

Whereas the grandparents of contemporary college students feared that absences equaled missed opportunities and subsequent failure, many of today's youth are confident knowing that if they were not there for it, it could not have been too important. And these students, we should remember, are those we have labeled as our best and brightest.

Chapter 9
WHAT'S FOR SUPPER TONIGHT, SON?

How did this happen? Here is a hint: it does not begin in college. American middle-class children are being raised and educated to believe the world waits for them. Anyone struggling to believe this need only examine the family lives of those with active, "successful" high school students. When is dinner? That depends on when practice ends. When is the dentist appointment? During English class, of course, otherwise the poor kid misses something important—something she does not want to miss.

Parents and educators, moreover, all too often play into the game of "do what you need to do when you need to do it." This is especially evident with the approach taken with our most talented youths. Adults reward them for their talents by excusing them from the mundane. This sounds ridiculous and impossible, yet any high school teacher reading this can relate to the frustration experienced when students miss class (sometimes for days) to decorate for the homecoming dance or prom.

And which kids are allowed out of class in high schools to hang posters and streamers? These are the great students, the student-council kids, the all-stars. When Johnnie and Wendy are excused from periods four through seven to decorate the auditorium, educators and parents too often forget that they are learning something from adults that day. They learn that showing up for work—showing up for something that is not fun—takes a back seat to fun.

There can be rewards in life for being a good, hardworking person. Perhaps this is what Johnnie and Wendy deserve for all of their effort in school. Perhaps. But the lesson extends well beyond the few students who miss classes for fun.

The other students learn during these moments as well. If rigor and expectations are scaled back on the days Johnnie and Wendy are decorating the float, educators are teaching the less popular students they are not important enough to miss class and, more significantly, they are not worthy of full attention when Johnnie and Wendy are absent. We shall continue with notes and assignments when all the great students have returned; for now, please find something to keep yourselves quiet.

A high school dean of students endured a knockdown, drag-out fight with a mother concerning an attendance issue with her daughter. The student missed the first four periods of the day, and her absences were deemed (by the dean) unexcused. The administrator's decision, according to the mother, was not only completely unfair but also outside of his purview.

For minutes the mom and the educator squared off on the issue. "You don't understand. It's not up to you. I have excused her for these periods!" The dean politely assured her he had no intention of dictating the policies within her home; however, the high school administration team, not she, determines whether or not an absence is excused in school.

What kept this girl out of school for the first half of the day? Did she have an appointment with a doctor? Was she feeling ill? Was she visiting Notre Dame or Harvard? Was the administrator overstepping his bounds and proving himself to be a first-class, power-hungry jerk? The girl was having her hair cut and styled. Prom was not too far away, and the stylist "only has so many openings." A girl needs to do what she needs to do.

ALWAYS LEARNING

Parents, teachers, and administrators must recognize that students are always learning something. Remembering this can help adults avoid inadvertently teaching young people habits that will eventually hinder their ability to succeed.

What happens in classrooms when the most popular kids roll in late—even if just a few seconds—and the class is therefore delayed? Is it funny? Do teachers joke around with these kids, thankful to have them present for the day's lesson? Is the tardiness consistent? If it is, the lesson is deplorable: *cool people, good looking people, talented people do not need to work as hard as everyone else. Furthermore, the rest of us wait for them.*

What about the approach to educating when the band kids—or the choir kids—or the student-council kids are absent for a school-sponsored activity? Do classes shut down while remaining students watch a movie during those periods, or do teachers forge ahead with lessons about coordinating conjunctions and dividing polynomials? Did the band kids miss anything when they were gone? If not, an opportunity to teach something vital was missed.

Every year, countless school districts send teams to compete for a state championship. The look of the classrooms one full day ahead of the game is often conflicting for teachers. With half the students absent, presumably due to the game, instructors weigh their options. What should students do? I mean, half of them are gone!

Indeed, half the students are sitting in their desks—and every kid in the school, present or not, will learn something important within the next few days. If school has not been canceled (this is another issue altogether), public educators owe it to everyone to ensure that absent students actually miss something they will need to make up and for which they will be held accountable.

What is being taught if this does not happen? *Rich kids, those with parents who can afford to send them to a state tournament and the associated hotels and restaurants, are the only students worthy of our full, undivided attention.*

Educational leaders are called to rethink many of the practices, silent or not, defining students today. Again, what are responsible adults teaching? Because, whether adults think it is happening or not, students are always learning.

What is being taught, therefore, when almost every period of a school day is interrupted by an announcement from the office? The voice from above reminds students, in stereo, that the lunchroom salad bar is closed until Wednesday, that the Chamber Orchestra students are to pay Mr. Hoff their transportation fee, and that next Friday is "dress like your favorite superhero" day.

Meanwhile, the *time* that should be spent on work is being spent listening to Big Brother and subsequently reeling everyone back into academia after the announcements. What are we teaching when we do this day after day? *There is always something more important than this obligation right here, right now.*

Trouble believing this? Try walking into the middle of the football practice field or the basketball court to remind student athletes the salad bar is unavailable until Wednesday. See what happens. What we value is reflected by how we respect it with our timeliness and attention.

Right here, right now. The best teachers establish their classrooms as the "right here, right now" capital of the world. There may be fun and exciting things going on outside of the classrooms of the best teachers, but their students will not be participating in these ventures until the work is done. And if class was missed by Johnnie and Wendy? These two youngsters will be required to catch up. And they had better catch up soon—because the best teachers always have a bunch of stuff to cover and not nearly enough time in the day to cover it.

SO WHAT DO WE DO ABOUT IT?

The school day is the greatest opportunity in the world to teach timeliness and attendance. If teachers are wise, everything they do can lend itself to keeping a schedule and working diligently within it. A few simple guidelines can go a long way toward teaching young people the value of time. These are nothing magical or groundbreaking. The best teachers have been using these teaching philosophies related to time management for decades.

1. Teach students the necessity of being on time—all the time.

    Great teachers accomplish this with their students. Showing up late for Mr. Tack's class is the equivalent of spitting in his face. He has an English lesson to teach, it is incredibly important, and unexcused tardiness is completely unacceptable in his world. And this is exactly why students are not tardy for Mr. Tack's class without a very good excuse.

What teachers do with their fifty minutes a day had better be important enough to insist on timeliness from their students. This habit alone is an education as important as the curriculum for which educators endlessly test.

2. Teach students the value of every day.

   Most of the potential pitfalls for preservice teachers have been addressed by the time they are scheduled for student teaching. These individuals have passed the necessary tests, they have likely experienced success within their practicum experiences, and they have maintained the academic requirements determined by their college or university.

   There are instances, however, that expose a choice few teacher candidates as incapable of continuing within the profession. What is the most common reason for failing at this point? Are they lacking in content knowledge? Is their classroom management atrocious? Do they just hate kids? No, incredibly, the most prominent reason for concern with future teachers is their inability to string together five days in a row of actual work.

   Far too many young people have been raised and educated to believe that success is found within a fifteen-minute rock-star performance. I was fantastic in class on Monday, why would you feel the need to call on me Tuesday?

   There is nothing flashy about the "every day"; it is often boring and people almost never receive a trophy for it. However, today's young people should be reminded that an "every day" emphasis is exactly why successful people have almost everything they need and a great deal of what they want.

   Every day. The best teachers educate every day. The side effect of this, it must be remembered, is that the students in these courses learn the value of working every day.

3. Teach students how to use the time.

   In truth, being on time and attending with consistency is merely the recipe for mediocrity. The most successful, the decision makers, the award winners, separate themselves by using their time better than those around them.

   How do they do it? This seems to be the question educators ask without careful consideration. The most successful students, those who can juggle academic accomplishment alongside extracurricular involvement, are usually gifted with intellect and ability. Along with these, and sometimes instead of these, however, they have been taught to make the most of their time.

   It is a mistake to perceive students' time-management skills as inherent, not too different than one's height. Further, it should be remembered that honor roll students who play three sports, sing in the choir, and volunteer at the Humane Society were raised by parents who were not afraid to make their kids mow the lawn after football or volleyball practice.

Staying up late to study for a chemistry quiz (see also, doing homework) does not require talent; it is a habit that is simply reinforced by the successes associated with "using the time." Want to play basketball while also being a violinist for the school orchestra? Great, that means homework is completed when other kids are watching television, playing on the computer, or sleeping. This, educational leaders must somehow get through their thick skulls, is what the best parents teach.

Educators should be emulating the best parents and their methodology, which creates the most accomplished students. Why resist? Does anyone think student success amounts to luck? Skilled teachers know better. What are students learning if they have five hours every evening available for television, video games, or their smart phone? This is all too often why students (at least the privileged middle-class kids) do not have time for homework.

Many school districts across the country are striving to eliminate homework. Instead, some modern education reformers suggest teachers grade what needs grading—tests, for example—and disregard the unnecessary mess of everything leading up to these. After all, why bother with the means if the students eventually find the end?

This is a horrible, stupid mistake. Yes, there are realities that keep many children from completing their homework to satisfaction. Yes, educational leaders ought to recognize that homework, at least for some students, is a monumental task. That admitted, K–12 experts should also recognize that homework has for decades been accomplishing endlessly more than what some believe. It has been teaching children how to spend time on something for the purpose of succeeding.

The parents of the best students know very well why adults should bother with the means—because the value found within the means is endlessly more important than the temporary accomplishment of standardized-test accomplishment. Further, if impressive students can "thrive" academically without putting in the time, K-12 leaders should be wondering why we dare label it success in the first place.

WHAT MAKES GREAT?

Time spent on something is an education in itself. Inexplicably, school districts often casually avoid this truth. Honestly, how did anyone get good at anything? They put in the time.

The 10,000-hour rule has become a relatively well-known maxim in society. In short, the notion is that 10,000 hours are required at something for one to be deemed an expert in that endeavor. This rule must be applied with the assumption that the time used toward the activity, performance, or project is used with great purpose and with the goal of being excellent. Great coaches, for example, will remind that practice does not make perfect—perfect practiced makes perfect.

Public school teachers, with an estimated 180 student contact days a year, need nearly seven years of experience in the classroom to amass 10,000 hours as an educator. Considering the fact that it may take a few years for a teacher to actually develop an educational identity worthy of fine-tuning, it can be argued that becoming an expert in education takes ten great years of teaching.

Most veteran teachers are willing to admit that it took a decade to achieve excellence consistently. Successful parents and educators know the value of putting in the necessary time to accomplish something impressive. We cannot possibly be the same people neglecting to teach our children how to show up on time and use every day to get better.

TEN
Work Ethic and Dedication

SOFT SKILLS

The September 2013 edition of *Educational Leadership* includes an interview with Angela Lee Duckworth, associate professor of psychology at the University of Pennsylvania. The article, titled "The Significance of Grit," examines the relationship between grit (defined as the ability to work hard at something and stick with it) and achievement.

In short, Duckworth explains that successful students—and people as a whole—are those who prove capable of both rebounding from setbacks and sacrificing distractions to accomplish something significant on a long-term basis. The basic principle is rather simple: we get better when we try harder.

This is news? Unfortunately. Public education in this country has fallen over itself measuring children via high-stakes testing; furthermore, habits like work ethic and dedication have been marginalized to the extent of being labeled "soft skills" by people who are perhaps too important to actually work with young people on a daily basis.

Any parent or educator willing to speak out against the values of work ethic and dedication is too daft for an audience. Yet somehow work ethic and dedication struggle for the attention they deserve. Why? K–12 state and federal government testing agencies have no interest in pulling back the curtain to face the real reasons too many young people are struggling in school and beyond. It takes courage, after all, to tell citizens that their children are failing because they have never learned to *work* for anything that did not reward them immediately.

Curriculum attainment is, ironically, more essential to the long-term success of young people than even the measure-mongers realize. Reading with a thoughtful and critical eye, writing properly and with purpose, and having at least a basic grasp of math and science are all vital for contributing in modern society. If a citizenry does not know anything, it seldom matters how hard it works.

The problem is only a small percentage of people learn anything significant without working hard—and therein lies the message experts in education must acknowledge. Dr. Duckworth beautifully communicates this reality in *Educational Leadership* by reminding us that kids do not learn complicated math because parents and educators emphasize complicated math. Kids learn difficult material because the adults in their lives have emphasized hard work and dedication; math success is simply a by-product.

TEACHING KIDS TO WORK

Years ago, a golf professional contacted his friend (a teacher) with an interesting request. The friend was a high school English teacher and coach at the time; subsequently, he was familiar with a great percentage of the adolescents within the community. The golf pro was looking for students to work in his shop and on the grounds crew during the summer months.

"I'm not looking for your 4.0 students," he said. "I need a couple kids who can actually get out of bed on a Saturday and come to work." Being an educator at heart, the English teacher defended the academically successful students. Sadly, however, he knew exactly why the golf professional spoke as he did. School success is too often disconnected from the expectations of successful people outside of academia.

The golf pro was confident that if his friend provided him with a few names of young people capable of looking and dressing appropriately, armed with enough personality to speak with adults without mumbling, and willing to get up early and work diligently, he could teach them whatever they would need to know and pay them handsomely in the process. He was right.

What is student success in schools if it does not translate to the world around us? Clearly, there is a problem when model students—those who have successfully navigated every assessment piece thrown their way—are belittled for their inability to get work done.

Colleges, universities, and the workforce only desire a few characteristics from young people: smart and hardworking. More importantly, if there is a choice to be made, the hardworking individual always wins. We can teach someone how to create a spreadsheet, ground a wire, write a short paper, or rotate the tires on a 2005 Honda Pilot; no one cares to teach a capable twenty-five-year-old how to work.

SCHOOL SHOULD BE DIFFICULT FOR EVERYONE

"I need a couple of kids who can actually get out of bed on a Saturday and come to work." These words from the golf professional are revealing on several fronts; they also hint at something pragmatists have been quietly thinking for years.

The assessment craze has created flaws within American schools; one of the most egregious errors centers on the fact that schools have now placed a collection of unimpressive finish lines within K–12 education. No Child Left Behind, Core Standards, AYP—these great ambitions are designed to pull everyone up. In many instances, admittedly, students have been raised up. Unfortunately, fewer and fewer of today's young people are capable of leaving anyone behind.

Why should they? They have the necessary test scores proving their adequacy, after all. Within school districts immersed in basic standard alignment, the brightest students are often coasting through their coursework. In many instances, the final two years of high school resemble a drive-thru service.

Countless communities have droves of seventeen- to eighteen-year-old boys and girls driving around town in the middle of a school day. Why? There is no need to fill their schedule every day, for they have reached the academic, standards-based finish line and there is apparently no concern from district administrators that more education is required.

This is problematic. Seventeen-year-old boys and girls with enough free time, in the middle of a Tuesday, to walk around the mall and swing by McDonald's for an afternoon snack should be an indication that their academic prowess is nothing short of elite. These young people should have Yale as a backup plan. Nope, they have merely met the needs of a minimalistic standards-based education within a school district that finds it easier to release adolescents from school at midday than to pay teachers to instruct them until 3:30.

Many parents find it difficult to allow their children to take "half days"; they insist their kids keep taking classes until graduation. Federal and state standards were never really in doubt with these people; their parenting standards reach far beyond accomplishing adequacy.

Regardless of the reason, whether it is school-budget related or an attempt to reward students for accomplishing something adequate, school administrators should be ashamed of themselves if they are excusing students from school with the message that they have already learned what needed to be learned.

Meanwhile, there are classmates of the mall cruisers who have significantly less free time on their hands. These students are struggling to meet the standards and often find themselves working diligently in school because of it. Public schools supplement the education these children receive; they grind away in English and math classes while being nagged by traditional classroom or special education teachers.

These kids are often called to work their tails off in school because it is necessary for them to represent themselves as adequately educated. Ironically, these are often the children who become successful after everyone stops measuring.

A measure-monger's mentality makes this reality possible. Finish lines—public education too often defines itself as a progression of finish lines. Somehow, leaders in education have lulled themselves into believing that an education can be measured while it is happening and that the ultimate goal is a graduation with minimal requirements met. The result of this emphasis is sobering: a high school diploma has become little more than a rite of passage for any student capable of reading and writing to any acceptable degree.

Why did the golf professional have no insistence for the honor roll students to work for him? Because he pays attention; he sees the honor roll students playing golf on his course after their school day wrapped up at 1:30. These kids may or may not be what he is seeking, but it will have nothing to do with their academic abilities. Can they work? This is the defining difference between successful and unsuccessful people, smart or not.

MISSION STATEMENT

All school districts have a mission statement, a vision for students and perhaps their relationship with the community surrounding them. The purposes for such a vision can vary; effective mission statements act as a lighthouse for educators. Am I acting in accordance with our mission statement? Are my students reflecting the values we have prioritized?

One school district applies the following mission: *All students will have the academic, social, and personal skills to be career, college, and community ready.* The associated district vision (for educators) reads: *Together, we inspire a passion for learning, discovery, and excellence.*

This mission is as good as any. Nonetheless, with the goal that youths will need to develop specific habits required for successes beyond the classroom, the following additional thoughts could be added to a typical district mission:

Together, we will teach young people the value of hard work and dedication.

Yes, possessing a *passion for learning, discovery, and excellence* is important. In fact, it is a perfect vision. But this is not found in a miracle or within the world's best lesson plan (nor is it found in the mall); a passion for excellence is learned when teachers demand work ethic and dedication from their students.

Want to be great at something, kid? Of course today's children want excellence. Everyone wants excellence. Teachers and parents are called to teach children how difficult excellence is to achieve. Further, responsible adults teach youths how rewarding it is to experience genuine accomplishment. This only comes from work.

Work. Want to be impressive? Want to be proud of something? Work. It is the only answer. Talent is common and shallow; it all too often promises what it will not deliver when it is needed the most. Talent is a gift. We have no business being proud of talent. Work. Dedication. Monday mornings. Five days in a row. When no one is there to compliment us. Scratching out the fifth revision of an essay before it is acceptable to present to the teacher. Work.

Great parents attempt to teach their children this. The best teachers are helping. Kids should look good, smell good, be respectful, and have the minimum academic skills too. None of this will matter, however, if responsible adults do not teach them the relationship between work and success.

Together, we will teach our children how to handle failure.

Failure is the ultimate F-word in schools. Many adults hide from failure, eliminating it from possibility and referencing it like death—a permanent mark on a child's soul. This is a mistake. Parents and educators should not strive to shield young people from failure at all costs; they should, moreover, teach these children what to do when they fail.

It is impossible for dedication to become a habit without failure. This truth is found nowhere easier than on college campuses. Professors working with freshmen can set their watches to the first request these students have for a meeting. It is about twenty minutes after their first test has been graded and returned.

One freshman student dropped by her adviser's office unannounced last spring. She took a seat, looked up at her, and the professor feared she was soon to hear about something horrible. This young woman looked devastated, like she was merely moments from completely unraveling. Honestly, the college teacher recalls wondering how to transition the student from her office to a crisis counselor. Something was obviously seriously wrong.

She received a C on her chemistry test. The professor waited for the rest. Nothing; she got a C on a test, and it had nearly placed her in rehab. We should remember that it is not necessary for some young people, especially our most academically talented, to earn an F to experience failure.

Clearly, we must also remember that every student must be taught how to handle whatever "failures" find them. Looking as though you just lost your parents in a plane wreck, moreover, is not an acceptable response to getting a C on a chemistry test.

"Are you a chemistry major?" The adviser knew this answer but needed to get the ball rolling somehow.

"No."

"Do you like chemistry?"

"No."

"Did you study hard for this test?"

"Yeah, I studied like crazy for that thing!" She went off with this. She was seething about her poor performance after giving it her all. There was a level of self-disgust, to be certain, but she maintained that she had given the test her full attention.

"So what's the problem?"

This young woman had never earned a C on anything, and the sky was clearly falling. The discussion took several different turns, ranging from how to study difficult material, whom to seek for assistance, and how we all have natural academic strengths and weaknesses. But the goal of the discussion, at least from the professor's perspective, was to make this young person approach her setback in a way she should have been taught years ago: *What now?*

The student was asked if she was planning on dropping out of college. Knowing the professor was not serious, the student transitioned from miserable to a bit annoyed. After enough trust was established and she assured her adviser she actually wanted advice, the educator poured it on her. "Stop crying; nobody died." This may be insensitive, but she needed a dosage.

"You did your best and you got a C. What are you going to do about it?" Educators cannot possibly wear out the question, "What are you going to do about it?" Successful people learn, more than anything else, to do something about what disappoints them.

How is it possible that a nineteen-year-old college freshman with average academic skills has never earned a C? How is it possible that an otherwise emotionally stable student is left mentally crippled in the wake of an average grade she earned in a class she finds difficult? The adults in her life did this to her. Otherwise responsible adults allowed her to get this far without ever having to ask, "What now?"

Failure, however each individual perceives it, happens. Failure is necessary. Today's children must scrape their proverbial knees, in and out of school, and responsible adults must teach them the value of "What now?"

Writing is the most readily available example of student failure and the subsequent need for "What now?" Many of these poor writers are, at least according to their transcripts, model students. Furthermore, most struggling writers, at least at the college level, express a sense of disbelief and regret that they have been academically successful while somehow not knowing how and when to punctuate a sentence using a semicolon and conjunctive adverb.

One young woman, tremendously academically successful, shared with an instructor that she usually avoids writing the word *however* in a sentence because she is fearful she will flounder with the associated punctuation.

Excuse me? How is this even remotely possible for students headed to our colleges and universities? Even for experts in education, the answer is confusing. Clearly, our students are not learning to write as well as we would hope. It makes sense, then, that this is a curriculum issue.

Perhaps. Many within education lament the dying breed of English teachers who demand proper sentence structure, punctuation, and clarity from their students' papers. They cringe at the thought of middle and high school language arts instructors (and all the other teachers) asking of their students to make a dozen posters to represent an alternative comprehension of the three-day movie they all watched in class.

There is more to poor student writing, however. Most college students assure us that they did, in fact, write papers in high school. Furthermore, an alarming number of college students share that they had never received anything but an A on a paper before entering college. This is where schools have failed students. An A on a paper containing four or five significant, distracting errors per paragraph? Ridiculous.

Almost all students are smart enough to correct poor writing; they simply need their parents and teachers to insist that they do. America's twenty-year-old college students are not struggling with punctuation and sentence structure because the concept is too difficult to grasp. In fact, most of them are astounded when they learn how simple it is to use *however* as a conjunctive adverb.

They struggle with writing because teachers too often do not insist upon making them write three or four drafts before they give the A, and even some impressive teachers are often deeply troubled by the notion of giving a bright student a C.

It would be difficult to prove that the most successful people are measurably smarter than those who surround them. Instead, it is more likely that successful adults have developed the incredibly valuable habit of reacting well to failure. They fight while others crumble, they feel challenged while others feel defeated, and while those around them chew their fingernails and concern themselves with what or whom to blame, the successful become almost impervious to anything that unnecessarily distracts them from being effective.

This is learned. We should be teaching it.

ELEVEN
Respect, Decency, and Humility

WHEN NO ONE IS LOOKING

"What's wrong today, Paul"

"Not happy today."

"Oh, I wish you were happy. I love to hear you sing when you are happy."

Paul was a special man who worked as a custodian for United Hospital in Grand Forks, North Dakota, while my mother was employed as a tumor registrar. Tumor registrars collect and organize data associated with cancer patients; my mom worked closely with the likes of surgeons, hospital administrators, cancer specialists from across the country, and Paul.

From time to time, we would hear about Paul and his singing, how he would showcase his voice while mopping and how my mom would stop and listen. There were days when Paul did not feel like singing, and those were the days she would nag him like no one else on earth could so that he would sing again. Mom would occasionally share these stories (she glowed when talking about Paul), and we received them with little effect. Seriously, who cares if you made the custodian sing?

I was barely out of college and at the beginning of my teaching career when my mother resigned from her post to accept a supervisory position for the state capital tumor registry in Bismarck, North Dakota. The administrators at United Hospital put together a retirement party for her complete with family, friends, colleagues, hot coffee, punch, and delicious cupcakes.

The event was well attended; I watched as she gracefully accepted congratulations and well-wishes (and a gift or two) from one impressive professional after another. It was truly no different from the dozens of retirement parties I have attended since that day; it was just fine—and likely soon to be forgotten. Then, with no warning whatsoever, my mother's retirement party became something few in attendance would ever forget.

Amid a sea of professionals dressed in business suits and scrubs, Paul walked into the conference room with a frightening look of determination. Clearly on a mission, he paused and scanned the room, and upon finding his target, he resumed his march. He was wearing a custodian uniform, and the sweat covering his face and shirt exposed him as a man who had been spending the day with physical labor. He worked his way to my mom, who looked like she always looks—impeccably professional and beautiful. They stood face-to-face.

Tears ran down Paul's sad face as my mom held her arms open to hug him. The hug had to wait. With every set of eyes in the room staring, Paul started to sing. Although the emotions of the moment caused his voice to waiver, the room was filled with his incredible song. The rest of us were silent, awestruck. Never looking away from my mother, he sang the entire piece through his tears. After the last amazing note could not be held another moment, my mom wrapped her arms around the man—and every person with a soul was wiping tears.

Who is this guy? What had just happened? How in the world did this developmentally disabled man, a custodian, have a relationship with a woman who looks like she lives and works seven million miles away from him? She loosened her embrace, took his hands, and urged him to dry his eyes because, after all, she prefers him when he is happy.

Every United Hospital employee in that room walked by Paul on a daily basis. They had all heard him sing. It is impossible to know, of course, how many people at the hospital made a connection with this man. What is certain, however, is that no one in that company had ever seen (or heard) anything like that in their entire life. It was not pathetic. It was not odd. It was not unfortunate. It was nothing short of beautiful. It was a perfect reflection of who and what the best people should be.

What makes a man enter a party unannounced, risking embarrassment and complete failure, to sing a song of thanks for a woman he barely knows? This behavior stemmed from being respected. My mom made Paul feel valuable—not once with a pat on his shoulder while her boss was watching, not with patronizing chatter delivered without so much as looking at him—but by stopping, every day, and talking to the man when no one was looking and nothing could be gained.

It is likely that the events of that day shamed some people. How is it possible, one could wonder, that she has established a relationship with this man, to this extent, while most people had been too busy, too important to learn that she has two children and a miniature schnauzer named Colonel Potter?

I am grateful to have witnessed that moment at the beginning of my professional career, for there were lessons to be learned that day. Respect? Decency? If the only people receiving these from me are those I need to impress, I am empty and pathetic. And humility? This is what reminds us we are not too important to stop and talk to the man who is mopping our floors.

GOOD PEOPLE

It is easy to believe that good people—respectful, decent folks who carry themselves with an aura of humility—are simply born that way. It is difficult to imagine that such people were ever knuckleheads. Likewise, it is convenient to think that disrespectful, selfish people are the result of genetics.

It is tempting to believe that all of us—the great citizens, the evil people, and the vast majority in the middle—are as we are because of nothing more than chance. Those great students in third-period AP English? Good luck. That crew we struggle to survive every day during fifth-period Grammar and Composition? Bad luck.

Nonsense. Aside from issues outside of our influence (severe mental illness, for example), people become who they were raised and educated to become. Students? They are a reflection of their parents' and teachers' expectations. It is not merely good fortune that has given my mother the decency to befriend a complete stranger; she likely had this modeled for her throughout her life. Luck, if it exists, is found in the fact that impressive role models were available for her when she was learning how to be an adult—and that these people cared enough about her to teach her respect, decency, and humility.

Behavior—good, bad, and otherwise—is learned. It would be wonderful, furthermore, if every child in public schools was gifted with a morally sound, high-character mother and father. The job of teaching would be much easier if respect, decency, and humility came with the child, if these children were raised to be good.

Public schools would be redefined if all children were raised to understand the connection between their attitude, their behavior, their decisions, and their ultimate success in life. It would be much easier to teach kids if all parents were like the best of parents.

This is not the case, unfortunately. In fact, there is a growing concern within the teaching profession that the number of positively influential families is shrinking. Whether this is a reality or not, educators are lying to themselves if they somehow maintain they have not inherited the ever-increasing job of teaching young people how to be decent and respectful.

Here is something to remember: a great number of strong, impressive, decent adults were jerks as children and adolescents. The reason they are no longer intolerable? The strong, impressive, decent adults in their lives worked on them until they became tolerable.

Great parents and educators are called to be the influential adults. "Measurable" curriculum defines public educators for "experts" who would be incapable of supervising a middle school dance, yet a teacher's true calling reaches well beyond what can be tested. Respect, decency, and humility absolutely can be taught in schools. These values—habits—can and should be emphasized at every turn within public school classrooms, hallways, lunchrooms, and gymnasiums. If educators turn their backs on this issue, they are communicating to children that talent and the associated results are the emphasis.

NARCISSISM

Talent is luck. Six feet five, great hand-eye coordination, fast as a spooked deer, and capable of jumping out of the gym? These traits are not coached; talent is what one is given. Yet countless adolescents meeting these descriptions are treated like royalty in schools. It is oftentimes nothing short of embarrassing how schools take care of kids who can dribble a basketball, throw a football, or shoot a puck. Adults are drawn to youth talent—especially athletic talent—like mosquitoes to a bug zapper.

They are the Friday-night heroes; these kids are more recognizable than most mayors. In many instances, great high school athletes are the symbols of communities. They are interviewed for the newspaper, they have an entire section of the nightly televised news dedicated to their hobbies, and parents and educators have all too often fallen into a trap of treating them like they have developed a cure for cancer.

The adoration of impressive high school student athletes is a great example of adults teaching youths by what is emphasized. At best, these athletes are truly hardworking, high-character kids (and many are), and they are made to feel rewarded for such traits. This is not always the case, however. Countless athletes are under the impression that their worth is associated with their talents alone; moreover, their nonathlete classmates agree.

School districts provide student activities, groups, and exclusive clubs for the growth of children. Sports, of course, are the most common. We celebrate student athletes—and we should. Yet what is being emphasized with these young people often leaves them misguided.

High school sports have become a breeding ground for narcissism among our adolescent student athletes. At their core, youth sports are being wounded by self-love and a lost perspective. Student athletes, especially boys, can be found believing they have accomplished incredible feats while, in fact, they may be accomplishing nothing of the sort.

Further, many of these kids now believe their lives as high school athletes are far more important than academic success; the well-being and success of classmates, teammates, and peers; or the lives of their own family members. In reality, the vast majority of these student athletes are average at best. An alarming number of high school athletes, however, have the ego of Michael Jordan while possessing barely enough skill to be a role player on a college intramural squad.

Is there any mystery as to how this trend happened? If high school student athletes believe their sporting lives are more important than the lives of their moms, dads, and anyone else, it is likely because that belief has become a reality. Adolescent athletes have somehow dictated when mothers and fathers can take vacations, when and if supper will be served on schedule, and whether or not happiness is allowed for a twenty-four-hour period after every game.

Many of these student athletes actually believe they will receive a scholarship to play college sports while at the same time being too short, too slow, and too uncoordinated to be a good player on their high school varsity team. And while all this is happening, the stuff these kids should be focused on regarding college—studying, for example—is being profoundly neglected.

The amazing part about narcissism in high school sports is not that there are student athletes who have grandiose perceptions of themselves, but rather that more of them do not. Adolescents have an incredible ability to keep their peers grounded, and this is exactly why many, if not most, high school athletes are more humbled and realistic among their peers than they are with members of their family and educators. Further, the trend of being an adolescent superstar in one's own home is relatively new. In the not-too-distant past, moms and dads were not in the habit of anointing their adolescent sons and daughters as high school athlete royalty.

Although the easiest and most prevalent example available, youth sports is not the only instance of adults praising talent (whether it is abundant or not) over genuine accomplishment.

Students absolutely should experience success within athletics and other organizations; furthermore, adults should be recognizing these young people for their (hopefully) healthy, positive contributions within our schools.

Responsible adults have no business being members of their fan club, however. Talented children want us to recognize them for everything they naturally do well. What students—all students—need from adults, however, is something far more beneficial than glowing adoration for their ability to score touchdowns.

WHO GETS NOTICED?

Who and what gets noticed within schools? If it is talent alone, educators are not teaching effectively. Students need great parents and teachers to further recognize what requires no talent. Why? Love of talent alone leads to narcissism, plain and simple.

Great parents, administrators, and teachers can change that; they can provide avenues for talented students, of course, but there is an opportunity within public schools to *notice* something far more important. Public schools are filled with great kids who are not six feet five inches tall, athletically gifted, musically gifted, or otherwise noticeable to the outside world. Responsible adults can begin to teach respect, decency, and humility by rewarding students who display these characteristics.

Charged with improving the "climate" and "culture" of a school, one administrator attempted to think outside the box related to student recognition. There was a palpable absence of character in the classrooms and hallways of this school. Student–teacher and student–student relationships had deteriorated to the point where detention and suspension were both common and ineffective. If respectful people are not leading (or noticed) within a school, other people are leading.

"Other" people were leading this school, and they were receiving nearly all of the attention. What this administrator noticed was a school reflecting many struggling communities. There were highly recognized, successful students who played sports, sang in the choir, played in the band; they were the face of the school. Parents and teachers alike raved about them.

The school also contained struggling students who challenged the faculty and administration to the edge of their breaking points. These kids (as many as or more than the most impressive students) were disassociated with school rules, norms, expectations, and seemingly anything aligned with what responsible adults would describe as successful. These students were the reason the administrator was hired.

And then there was the bulk of the children, the vast majority of the student body who would neither be the focus of a pep rally or the reason for a police liaison officer working full-time on campus. These students attended school rather anonymously, involved in some degree with one activity or another but seldom receiving attention for either excellence or delinquency. This concerned the effective educators to no end; when a respectful, decent, and humble student goes unnoticed in school because she is neither on probation nor capable of shooting three-pointers, something needs to change.

Improving school culture does not happen with the wave of a wand, and it certainly does not happen overnight. The administrator's first several months were spent chasing student drug dealers. He vowed to make his school more comfortable and inviting for the majority by making it the most uncomfortable, miserable environment possible for any students hoping to buy or sell drugs on campus. He knew every police and parole officer by name, and they were all kept busy.

Although it is almost impossible to ensure a complete victory with such missions, the attack on drugs and other ganglike junk was truly successful. Teachers, administrators, and even concerned parents worked to clear the hallways during class time, rid the school of scary "hot spots," and make the school environment safer and more inviting for anyone not looking for trouble.

This work only goes so far, however. Feeling safe in school should be an assumption, not a grand victory. By taking ideas from several other schools with which he was familiar and subsequently creating a workable, affordable idea for his own school, the high school administrator introduced "Pride of Pirates" (after the school mascot)—the students eventually began calling it "POPS."

POPS was incredibly simple. When the idea began, he sent an email to all teachers asking them to nominate one student for the current nine-week quarter with the following qualities:

- Respect
- Decency
- Humility
- Responsibility
- Work ethic
- Other traits we hope to recognize within our school

The high school administrator reminded teachers that talent was not one of the criteria and that the goal of POPS was to recognize what too often has been ignored. He urged them to consider recognizing the good qualities of students who could truly benefit from having someone catch them being good. After a few days and a few dozen reminder emails to the slow teachers, the first POPS nominees were secured.

The immensely talented art teacher on staff created a fancy Pride of Pirates certificate, including background art and snazzy penmanship detailing the student's name and the name of the teacher who nominated him or her. The certificate was mailed home.

POPS nominees were called to the commons area and informed that next Wednesday they would be treated to pizza for lunch at Happy Joe's (a local pizza place with unbelievably good pizza). An administrator and a few additional chaperones would take them on a bus, they could eat all they wanted from the buffet, and the school would pay for it. When that day came, every nominated student loaded onto the bus.

The view from the front of the bus amazed this administrator. Brown kids, white kids, rich kids, poor kids, students who had three weeks remaining on a twelve-month probation sentence (honestly) were seated across from students who practice cello at 5:30 a.m. so they could clean their church before school. He stood facing all of them, and they looked like children—little, funny-looking, innocent children. The educator wondered how he could ever allow any of them to ruin his day.

"As most of you know, and some of you really know, I am Mr. Tufte." The kids on probation let out a great hoot. "If you are sitting on this bus, it is because one of your teachers was impressed with you and wanted to reward you for good behavior." They were silent; some were probably shocked. "All I ask is this: enjoy yourselves, eat well, be respectful to the people at Happy Joe's, and most importantly, I ask that you thank the person who nominated you for this."

Pride of Pirates evolved from that first round. An English teacher came to the administrator's office a few days after the first POPS luncheon and told him, with tears in her eyes, about the young man who thanked her for his nomination. Why was she crying? Because the student cried when he thanked her. It meant that much to him.

When the next quarter was coming to an end and before he could find the time to craft another fabulous email to the faculty, one of the school secretaries poked her head in his office and announced, "I want to nominate a kid for POPS this quarter." Her words filled the man with both joy and a profound sense of humility. How is it possible that he failed to involve secretaries, custodians, cooks, and paraprofessionals with an idea designed to recognize the unappreciated? His subsequent emails found more than just the teachers.

Soon there were more POPS students loading the bus (a bigger bus) for Happy Joe's. Can the school cooks tell us which kids are respectful and which need work? The administration team found out. Can the custodians? One custodian came to the office wanting to learn the name of a student. Because it was known where the young lady had her locker, the custodian and the principal decided to track the kid down during passing time. She was not in trouble; rather, she was witnessed reprimanding a younger student for neglecting to find the garbage can with his trash. The boy listened. The girl? Nominated for Pride of Pirates by the custodian.

SMALL STEPS

The goal of POPS—or whatever fun idea educators could develop—must go beyond simply rewarding students for being good people. After all, children should not grow up believing they have earned a free lunch for being decent and respectful; they should be decent and respectful because it is the right thing to do.

Pride of Pirates was, in some ways, a gimmick, but it accomplished something important. Starting with faculty, and eventually spreading to nearly every adult in the school, adults began to emphasize respect and decency by both recognizing it in students and demonstrating it themselves.

A veteran male teacher shared something interesting as it related to recognizing students for their respect and decency. "You know, it's a little harder to be my usual sarcastic, grumpy, and inconsiderate self in class when I know I need to nominate some kid for being good." There is obvious humor in a statement like this, but anyone who has ever taught knows the hidden truth behind the power of modeling habits.

Young people learn how to become good. We can model it for them, we can point it out when we see it, and we can correct disrespectful behavior whenever possible.

TWELVE
Responsibility and Teamwork

DELAYING GRATIFICATION

With the possible exception of the poorest among them, the nation's children are accustomed to having almost everything they want when they want it. This is a frightening trend. Furthermore, it leads to an uncomfortable reality for the nation's youth: unless a great deal is changed with the way adults are raising and teaching young people, today's children have very little chance of living better than their parents.

Why? Too many parents and other role models, including educators, are proving to be uninterested in providing two child-rearing essentials:

1. Saying no.
2. Teaching the relationship between responsibility and long-term success and fulfillment.

Young people are under the impression that successful elders somehow made a fortune (years ago) when no one was looking. They respectively worked as contract plumbers, registered nurses, public school teachers, civic engineers, and truck drivers, and their salaries must have been nothing short of fantastic. What else could explain their current lifestyle—the home, the lake cabin, the cars?

Successful grandparents have all of their nice stuff, along with a substantial savings account, because they were raised to understand that life can turn on a dime and present unforeseen challenges. They grew up hearing stories about the Great Depression and how foolish it is to live irresponsibly. They have spent most of their lives living with less so that they are never forced to live without. In short, they were raised and educated to delay their gratification.

Successful seniors are often proud to remind anyone willing to listen about the days of living in a one-bedroom, one-bathroom rented basement while sharing a hunk-of-junk car and never eating at restaurants. There was a television, but it had three black-and-white channels, and they were usually too busy to watch it. There was a telephone, of course, but it was plugged into the wall and almost never used. Rarely was there a need to chat with friends once one was home, they remind.

Things were simple for Grandpa and Grandma years ago; sometimes things were even difficult. This is why for a decade Grandpa worked a second job stocking shelves at the liquor store. Children (and many adults) need to be taught that this is why and how Grandma and Grandpa have the comforts they now enjoy.

Is this out of line? Is it unfairly judgmental of young people and their parents to assume they are not headed toward successful endeavors while too fondly describing the responsibility and character of elders? Is it overly gracious to assume greatness from our grandparents' bank accounts? Perhaps, but we should consider our opinions on this topic as they relate to a very common, realistic potential.

What happens when an extra five hundred dollars becomes our possession? Five hundred dollars is substantial for most people, and finding this much money (or having it automatically deposited via a tax return) is a blessing. Responsible people, regardless of their age, view this extra funding as an opportunity to pay a bill. If that is not necessary, they likely consider saving or investing the money.

Depending on the circumstances, spending five hundred dollars on toys is not necessarily irresponsible. If the bases are covered and the bills are paid, who is to say we cannot buy toys with our newly attained loot?

But a great percentage of American children are learning how to spend money by watching adults who do not have their bases covered or bills paid. An extra five hundred dollars? This is a new flat-screen television instead of fixing a leaky patch on the roof. This is a new gaming system, an iPad, and a skateboard instead of paying for school lunch and the fee for high school sports participation. These examples are not hyperbole; countless stories like this can be shared within any public school district in the United States.

Keep a leaky roof yet buy a new television? There are adults teaching this brand of responsibility. This example may be the extreme, and most may be capable of recognizing its insanity. Yet most responsible adults recognize a neighbor kid, a middle-class high school student with average academic ability (according to his mother), driving to school in a late-model Chevy Tahoe while barely seeing the road because his eyes are glued to a smart phone. It is rather evident that children learning to delay gratification are rare in all zip codes.

What can responsible adults do about it? Teaching children to delay gratification is not done with a quick lesson about money, possessions, and work. Delaying temporary gratification for the sake of long-term success is accomplished by teaching young people about responsibility and their obligations to everyone else on the team (the rest of us).

Showing off a new two-hundred-dollar skateboard and a fresh, sassy tattoo two minutes before asking the high school activities director to waive a fifty-dollar participation fee is grounds for a free life lesson about responsibility. Anyone thinking this example is an exaggeration need only chat with a school administrator.

We owe lessons like these to today's young people, for not many outside of some schools (or perhaps the federal government) will embrace the idea of paying for someone's roof while they are busy shopping for a new television.

REDEFINING TEAMWORK

Air travel is interesting for several reasons. Aside from the extraordinary opportunity to view humanity at its worst (see chapter 8) and an ever-increasing temptation to wear a hazmat suit to protect one from the germ party on board, there is also intrigue to be found in the safety instructions communicated prior to takeoff.

Passengers are reminded that, in the event of a loss of cabin pressure and, subsequently, necessary oxygen, we should address our own needs first (the words "for those who are able" are used) via the margarine-cup face mask. When that task has been handled, we can assist those around us.

The image of ourselves gesturing "simmer down" to our children as they panic and gasp for air? "Patience, children, I need to get this sucker strapped on." This notion is simultaneously hilarious and horrifying, yet there are lessons to be learned within the airplane oxygen mask guidelines.

For starters, we should meet our own needs whenever possible. This way of thinking was once common; however, today's children are all too often exposed as unwilling to confront anything significant when they suspect someone else could do it for them. Consequently, many young people are finding it difficult to meet their own needs and almost impossible to help anyone else.

Connecting the dots from here is not a strain. Today's youths pass on taking responsibility because many adults insist on it. If it is difficult, if it could result in a setback, or if it is feared children will not be pleased, misguided adults assume their responsibilities. Adult role models often think nothing of these small gestures, but these become the habits children learn. Teamwork? It begins with responsibility.

My neighborhood includes several families with teenage sons and daughters. These adolescents appear to have a comfortable life—leather-seated Chevy Tahoes and lightning-fast smart phones are subtle reminders.

One small example involves the detail of cutting the grass. Except for the children within one family, no young people mow the lawn in this neighborhood. In fact, a few of these folks pay lawn-care specialists to cut the grass—every week—from May to October. The lawn-care folks return in the winter to shovel for these families, too. This neighborhood is not a gated community; public school teachers live on this street.

This reality was a struggle to comprehend until a father explained his unwillingness to insist on or allow any of his three adolescent boys to mow the lawn. This man, a teacher, explained that he truly cherishes a well-kept lawn. He does not ask his boys to cut the grass because, quite frankly, they would not complete the job to his standards. He shared this with pride.

Seriously. Logic like this is almost too flawed for a response, and the fact that he is a teacher only enhances the unfortunate irony. This man has high standards for his yard; he likely has high standards for most things. How did this happen? How did he ever learn to crosscut his grass and trim around the trees to the point where it looks like a cover of a lawn-and-garden magazine?

More importantly, why in the world is he not teaching his three boys how to do this work with crazy-high standards? The ridiculous irony in a story like this is that his boys, endlessly more important than the yard, are learning the polar opposite of what their father values. We could be tempted to believe that children would see their parents work and see the beauty of the finished product and subsequently learn the value of responsibility.

This could happen. More than likely, however, the three adolescent boys, along with the crew of teenagers living in the neighborhood described above, are learning something far simpler. Because it needs to be done well, we kids will not be asked to cut the grass or shovel the driveway. Further, we will not be asked to learn how to do it well. Good teammates do not come from this line of thinking.

A family of six lives within this neighborhood. The four boys, ranging from fourth grade to high school junior, are constantly on the move. They play sports, they are involved in Boy Scouts, they blow stuff up in their backyard, and they likely even complete their homework now and then. The two oldest have started a small business out of their garage.

After finding customers by knocking on every door within walking distance of their home, the two boys spent their entire summer doing yard work for anyone (typically older folks) willing to pay their modest fee. They literally walk their own mowers down the street to their job sites—and, yes, they mow their own lawn too. Despite the fact that his father drives a fancy new four-by-four truck, the oldest boy rattles down the street in a vehicle that looks like it was unearthed at the local landfill. This is what creates good teammates.

Thirty years from now, our children should perceive themselves as the responsible adults capable of both securing their own airplane face masks and, if necessary, helping those around them.

DECISIONS DEFINE SUCCESS

Responsibility, in essence, is what people do when given an opportunity to choose. Children struggle with responsibility, in part, because adults have often only provided them with comfortable choices. Deciding between Applebee's and Buffalo Wild Wings on a Friday night is not a significant, thought-provoking life lesson in the waiting.

Responsible adults owe children the skill of responsible decision making. Effective parents typically begin this process with very simple yet highly significant lessons. Here are some classic examples:

- If you want that stuffed animal you have been talking about, you will brush your teeth every night.
- If you want video games you cannot afford, you will consistently make your bed and clean your room.
- If you wish to continue to eat for free in this home, you will help clean the kitchen after dinner.
- If you enjoy driving a car you did not buy with insurance you have not provided (notice a theme yet?), you will maintain the agreed-upon high school GPA and not once get in a vehicle with anyone who has been drinking.
- If you are strong enough to safely push a vacuum, a lawn mower, or a shovel, you will.

These are easy to the point of being predictable, yet moms and dads are failing at every turn with this opportunity. A high school kid refusing to study and consequently performing poorly in school while racking up enough hours on a cell phone to make Paris Hilton blush? How is this even remotely possible?

Adults teach children how to make responsible (and irresponsible) decisions. These choices are what they/we/all of us become. Experienced educators find it easy to identify students who are accustomed to making responsible decisions. These students and athletes are not great decision makers because they are smart kids with impressive academic and extracurricular resumes; they are kids with impressive academic and extracurricular resumes because they were taught how to make good decisions.

If it becomes a habit, the ability to make responsible decisions can follow someone for the remainder of his or her life. Long after a young woman has forgotten how to isolate the x in a complicated mathematical equation, she will remember to think things over before pressing "send" on a professional email written in haste and anger. Instead of charging everything to a credit card, she will save for three months to afford her girls' trip to Vegas. When she gives her word to her family, her friends, or her colleagues, it will mean something. This will not happen as a result of talent; she learned this responsibility.

THE ROLE OF SCHOOL

School is the perfect place to teach responsibility and teamwork. Hallways, classrooms, lunchrooms, and playing fields are microcosms of society; furthermore, educators are being neglectful if they fail to teach young people how to take care of themselves while living harmoniously with others.

The conversation of responsibility begins with academics. It is irresponsible to graduate capable high school students unable to read and write with modest effectiveness. Educators have failed when students somehow enter the workforce or college without possessing the capabilities required for minimal success. Genuine responsibility as it relates to academic progress, however, stretches beyond minimal success.

At a time in American education defined by achieving adequacy, great teachers nonetheless demand excellence from their students. What, exactly, is academic excellence? Quite simply, it is more. Just as leaders in education should not conclude that students are stupid when the school or district fails to accomplish AYP, they should also avoid celebrating student adequacy when the measure-mongers give their stamp of approval.

More. A great teacher's job is to meet students (and their abilities) where they live and subsequently push them to learn, do, and be more. This is the heart of responsibility. When children are appropriately pushed to be better than they were yesterday, they find it easier to thrive as adults.

The same approach is taken with effective extracurricular activities. Success is not defined by beating crosstown rivals in the speech meet, or even by making it to the state finals in football. Success is found in the process of improving. Responsibility becomes a habit for young people when the focus is process—not the results deemed important by other people.

In fact, shallow successes (bright children on the honor roll and talented athletes with winning records, for example) often act to hinder the development of responsibility. It is irresponsible for a high school senior capable of a 4.0 GPA to earn honor roll status with a 3.0 while somehow benefiting from three hours of school release each day.

What in the world is this young person learning about life when he is allowed, or even encouraged, to carry a half load of academics as a high school senior? The lesson is simple and troublesome: if he does just enough to get by, he can have everything he wants (sports, music, dances, recognition, etc.) while still somehow earning a spot on the B honor roll. Doing just enough to get by has a way of coming back to bite people. Educators should not be in the business of rewarding this level of responsibility.

Along with having individual responsibilities via the concept of "more," teachers and administrators in K–12 schools can provide endless opportunities for our children to successfully coexist with others. American children should have the following taught and reinforced throughout their years in school:

1. You are as important as everyone else.
2. You are not more important than anyone else.

These two messages are at the core of belonging to a successful team. Educators owe it to children (and everyone else) to teach them they are never anonymous, that their contributions are essential, and that always waiting for other people to either make decisions or follow through will lead to being a victim. Moreover, children must learn from responsible adults that being a victim while being capable is unacceptable.

Simultaneously, responsible adults must teach the highly recognized children that their opinions, passions, and abilities do not excuse them from the mundane. These children should be assured that they still have room for improvement. With this, they (along with the rest of us) should be made to understand that the less-popular, less-adored, reflective kids have a way of surprising us in the future.

Today's children are owed the skills necessary to work well together. Public schools belong to all of us; the lessons learned should extend beyond what can be assessed with a test. Just as effective parents and teachers emphasize lessons on responsibility, educators are called to teach teamwork—and we are wise to remember that young people are always learning. The possibilities are endless, but the following is a great start:

- If you want access to an affordable school lunch, often with a tremendous variety of options, you will, as a student body, conduct yourselves with respectability and clean up your messes.
- If you want school dances and carnivals, you will steadfastly follow the few rules associated with these events. Furthermore, after the fun, you (not your parents) will clean the auditorium, gym, or dance hall.
- If you wish to continue participating in (playing or watching) sports in our school, you will conduct yourselves with class and dignity. All of us are responsible for our reputation.

- If you enjoy driving a car to school, you will hold yourselves responsible for auto safety on our campus.
- If you are strong enough to have an opinion, to complain about anything, including what you believe to be your rights, you are strong enough to be a leader.
- If you can walk, bend over, and use your hands, you can pick up trash and throw it in the can.

The best message sent by being a member of a team is both simple and unbelievably powerful. Further, it can be applied in every team setting imaginable—football teams, student council, drama club, students using the cafeteria, anyone in the hallway during passing time, students in our school. In a nutshell, everyone matters.

Any school district struggling to foster a belief that everyone matters has problems far more significant than failing AYP.

THIRTEEN
Perspective

SCOREBOARDS

Delivering a brilliant lesson after a disappointing loss is difficult for high school coaches to imagine, yet it is exactly what one legendary basketball coach in Minnesota accomplished a few years ago. Although a new hire within his school district, Gary was a veteran educator headed for Hall of Fame coaching credentials (as well as numerous other impressive accomplishments in education), and he was armed with a slew of youthful, ambitious, and terribly naïve assistant coaches.

His basketball team had just lost a closely contested Friday-night game against a great rival, and aside from the punched locker here, the thrown shoes over there, a few threads of vulgarity, and the faint sound of sniffling from heads covered in towels, there was nothing to be heard in the locker room. The players, and a few of the coaches, were devastated.

This scene was no different from countless high school sporting events. When the team wins? Turn up the locker-room stereo, high fives for everyone, and everything that matters in the world is aligned with perfect harmony. When they lose? Devastation.

"Come sit down and look at me for a minute." Gary, old enough to be his assistants' father and the players' grandfather, had seen enough. He looked remarkably calm after losing a heartbreaker in the final seconds.

"Any of you guys notice the pep band tonight?" The boys blankly stared at him. "I did. God, they're good. I don't care what anyone says; we have the best pep band in the state!" Anyone with a modicum of with-it-ness would have suspected a motive beyond Gary's appreciation for the pep band. His players, however, remained oblivious to the fact that they were about to have their proverbial boats rocked.

"You guys see the two girls in the band sitting in the corner? The girls who cannot sit in the bleachers? You know, those two gals next to Mr. Iverson? What do they play; one girl plays clarinet, right? What does the other girl play?" Gary looked right into the eyes of a team leader, and he wanted an answer.

The boy, also a member of the band, knew who the girls were and what instruments they played. Everyone in the locker room knew these girls; many of the boys had been going to school with these wonderful classmates for ten years. The girls loved basketball, and they almost never missed a game. They were both confined to wheelchairs.

"What do you suppose those girls would do for an opportunity to play like you boys played tonight . . . to run around on a Friday night with the whole town cheering for them . . . to have a chance at playing a game they love against a great team? What if they could feel what it's like to have the pep band play for them?" The sledgehammer had dropped. Likely a bit confused within a myriad of emotions, many of the boys lowered their heads to think.

"Look at me." Gary's voice was stern but calm. "You played your guts out; you tried your best—and you lost. You don't have to like it, but throwing stuff around? Swearing? Punching lockers? That's unacceptable. What would you think of yourselves if you knew those two girls saw you acting like this?" With that he finished. He spoke nothing about shots, rebounds, blocks, or turnovers. Those details would be covered during Monday's practice.

Gary was fond of talking to his players about "the big picture." This is not to suggest that he was lackadaisical about competition. On the contrary, he endlessly pushed players for effort and preparation—especially in practice. Practice time, he knew, was the only valid time for measuring improvement.

The best coaches are not gushing with pride after a lopsided victory over an inferior opponent, nor do they behave like an exhausted toddler when a superior team defeats their team. Genuine growth, they know, happens in practice. Game days? Game days are for parents and the reward players get for practicing. Yet there is absolutely no guarantee, despite tremendous improvement, that the hard work in practice will result in a win against an opponent.

This is perspective. This is why some Hall of Fame coaches will glow when talking about their 1994 team that finished 4–19. Perspective is an ability to see the bigger picture, to understand something beyond its outward appearances and simple descriptions. Furthermore, perspective is an awareness that the important stuff cannot be measured by a scoreboard, a test, or any other scale.

This line of thinking is not universal. In some locker rooms, high school athletes would be scolded for failing to display the appropriate misery associated with losing to a rival. In some circles, throwing shoes, punching lockers, and swearing only reinforces how much everyone "cared" about the game.

For many, the games are everything. These people have no significant role at any stage that does not have a scoreboard present. These are the *Friday Night Lights* fans, who do not see practices—and most certainly do not see some athletes struggling throughout the week to read and write at grade level.

Perspective, furthermore, is becoming the rare gem of both parenting and public education in our country. Far too many school leaders are not modeling their approaches after the best coaches. Instead, they are often fixated on a scoreboard that is likely not communicating anything these experts did not know well before the tests were given. In some ways, many educational leaders are no wiser about their approach to education than the scoreboard-infatuated fans the best coaches struggle to tolerate.

Great educators carry a calm, expert perspective in the arena of AYP, ACT, MAP tests, and the like. Young people (and our communities) need adults to be wise with their approach to educating them; they need their role models to be less concerned with the finish lines created by people who have never taught a class. They need grown men and women to facilitate more practices—serious, productive practices—and cut back on game days.

They need adults who understand that like high school sports, genuine growth as it relates to education happens before and after the test, not during. They need educators to teach them beyond the measurable here and now because, among a million other reasons, their lives after high school graduation will be littered with challenges requiring an ability to see the big picture.

TEACHING PERSPECTIVE

There are numerous definitions for *perspective*, and it is possible that the term becomes neutralized and insignificant without clarifying exactly what brand of perspective children should be learning in school. Perspective, then, is an ability to effectively evaluate something (or a situation) and judge it for its relative importance.

When youths are consistently asked (by wise adults) to consider the significance of situations, they further develop an ability *to understand*. From better understanding comes informed, improved decision making. Educators can provide opportunities to understand with the following realities:

1. Despite the measure-mongers' efforts, not all curriculum can be marginalized into a number two pencil and an oval.
2. An enormous amount of time in school is spent on noncurricular issues, and we should be using this time to teach.

What, specifically, should be taught? Teaching perspective to young people goes beyond offering a lesson here and there; the best educators emphasize perspective at every turn. The possibilities for providing a bigger picture for children are truly endless.

SPORTS

This chapter began with a story about high school sports. Youth sports, and the associated passions displayed by coaches, athletes, and their parents, are the perfect venue for an extreme dosage of big-picture realism. As this is being written, an advertisement for a new television series is running throughout the day and on several channels. *Friday Night Tykes*, a thrilling drama about little boys (and their parents and coaches) from Texas aspiring to be football stars, promises to take us behind the curtain to view the cutting-edge approach to raising great prospects.

The advertisements show dad–coaches screaming such inspirational messages as "I don't care how much it hurts!" and shots of parents videotaping practices from the sidelines. At first glance, it is tempting to believe the show has been created to expose this brand of behavior as crazy. Nope. The preview also shows ten-year-old boys hitting each other at full speed, complete with the intoxicating pad-on-pad sound effects and the jovial roars from other boys, the coaches, and parents. Sure, some viewers are to recognize this as craziness, but this show is being sold as the recipe for creating Adrian Peterson and Peyton Manning.

What is the problem with that? Adrian Peterson is nothing like regular children; he is six foot one with 220 pounds of muscle, and he runs the forty-yard dash in 4.4 seconds. Furthermore, whether he grew up playing *Friday Night Tykes* football or not, his body and its associated abilities have absolutely nothing to do with some dad–coach screaming at him twenty years ago. Peterson is a freak of nature—not unlike most great professional athletes the public watches on television.

Perspective. Within healthy communities, youth sports should have a tempered passion. Yes, adults can and should get excited about their children playing sports because it is fun for them and it is great practice for kids to commit to something. However, community members must hear from wise educators early and often that sports will never supersede a school district's first mission—to appropriately and adequately educate students.

This can be accomplished by reminding students and community members that for every Adrian Peterson and Peyton Manning, there are thousands of John Tuftes, who also stand six foot one and weigh nearly 220 pounds. He too loved sports as a child, and without parents and educators wise enough to recognize that short and slow is fairly common in America, it is possible he would be the village idiot yelling, "I don't care how much it hurts!" to his son while simultaneously videotaping practice. If moms, dads, and teachers are going to be intense about anything, they should start with reading and writing and critical thinking.

GRADES AND TEST SCORES

Grades and test scores are worthy of emphasis—right up to the point where the grades are posted. At that stage, what As, Bs, and Cs accomplish is heavily dependent upon the level of perspective students possess regarding what it is these grades represent. Most experienced educators have known this for a while, yet teachers too often struggle to have grades, test scores, and other assessments make sense for students.

What, exactly, is a grade? At best, it is an accurate symbol of what a student has learned or is capable of doing. Educators and educational institutions wisely use grades—and GPAs and certain tests—to inspire and reward student accomplishment. Colleges and universities, for example, proudly boast the minimum ACT scores for acceptance (although few of these schools actually follow through with these claims), and it is hoped that students will strive for academic accomplishment with the necessary "proof" of an impressive GPA and ACT score.

In many cases, the grade-and-test-score system works. Superior American students are taught to chase the better symbols and subsequently learn enough to perform well on the ACT. Because of a thoroughly developed habit to earn acceptable grades, these students typically end up in our college classrooms and often flourish.

The grade-and-test-score system is terribly misleading most students, however. Without proper perspective, focusing on the symbolism of grades and numbers on a test leaves young people in a state of half-truth about what they have learned and what they are capable of doing.

Public school teachers would be astounded at the percentage of elite high school GPA students (with decent ACT scores) who honestly cannot write a three-page paper in college without a two-page rubric and small-group assistance. For many of these students, academic excellence has been an exercise in checking off the necessary boxes and following a heavily structured blueprint for an A. When the blueprint is removed, some of the best and brightest are exposed.

Of equal interest are the rather average students (according to their high school scores and grades) who find themselves thriving in colleges, universities, and the workforce. Ironically, in environments where testing and grading become secondary to thinking, writing, presenting, and performing, many previously unassuming students fly past their high school honor roll classmates. This type of student, for one reason or another, has likely been thinking and learning all along without the desire to impress by chasing symbols and numbers.

Yes, grades and test scores are necessary. The educator's job as it relates to student success, however, is more complicated than making a grade scale and rewarding those who best accomplish. Young people deserve to learn the value of working toward a goal, and if they are capable of good grades and impressive test scores they should achieve them.

Whether they accomplish this or not, children also deserve to learn that the grade or score alone means nothing. These do not make us smarter or dumber or anywhere in between; they are the best attempt at a reflection of student learning. Real student learning? That is what students do with information after we stop measuring.

HOMEWORK

A recent trend in K–12 education would have teachers believe that assigning homework is counterproductive if not unfair for students. If it cannot be accomplished in school, it should not be expected that students learn it at home. After all, some students are too busy, some students have messy home lives, some students blah, blah, blah.

Perspective. Homework was never intended to be fresh academia students must teach themselves; it was meant to be practice. At its best, homework allows students to leave school on a Tuesday afternoon with a basic grasp of a concept and return on Wednesday morning with deeper understanding. This happens when the basic concepts can be applied to new situations and the student can confidently progress academically. With this understanding, homework can be effective in any academic subject.

Admittedly, some homework is truly poor. It can be time-wasting busywork, and it can drain students' academic souls. It should be remembered, however, that good teachers are not assigning bad homework. Bad homework derives from poor teachers; furthermore, the wretched homework is usually the only remnant of a poor teacher's class that sees the light of day. This alone is not reason enough to eliminate homework from the practices of K–12 schools, for if school administrators cannot address poor teaching (including homework), there are bigger problems than homework.

Students do not need to enjoy every piece of homework, and parents and teachers should not lose sleep over their displeasure. Further, aside from those children in special circumstances and situations that make homework impossible or largely impractical (good teachers know who they are), homework is a fantastic opportunity to teach young people the value of paying attention (in class) and applying themselves (out of class) when it matters.

SUCCESS

Whether examining the world of youth sports, the notion of grades and tests, or something as mundane as homework, using perspective often boils down to a simple question: what is the right thing to think or do?

Veteran teachers, those who have worked with students for over a decade, likely experience the benefit of students improving their curriculum-related abilities because of their participation in class. Experienced teachers are not fools, however, and they know that countless other teachers could have taught these students to equally accomplish everything related to this curriculum.

As great teachers evolve, they begin to teach more than Shakespearean sonnets and conjunctive adverbs. Every day places them in a position to work with up to 150 students, and not every child is blessed with a set of parents capable and willing to teach him or her how to be impressive. Teachers, therefore, absolutely must be capable and willing to teach young people how to be impressive.

What do we do, for example, when we notice a sixteen-year-old boy who behaves and at least appears to respect his male teachers while he inexplicably and blatantly disrespects his female teachers? Do we as male teachers roll our eyes and take pride in our natural classroom management skills while wondering what it is our female colleagues are failing to do?

Do we take the next step and offer our female colleagues advice on handling the boy in class? "Hey, you just send him my way when he acts up. We'll take care of that crap." Does the administration get involved to the point of giving the young man detention? Do we make life easy on all of us and simply keep him with male teachers? All of these approaches are common in schools, and there is a glaring fault behind every one of these strategies.

Whether he is a "good kid" or not, whether he knows it or not, the boy disrespects and mistreats women. This is problematic. This is also the best time in the world to help the boy see a bigger picture.

Teaching perspective to young people is a never-ending job, and sometimes it is rather uncomfortable. One high school teacher well remembers looking into the eyes of a young man and telling him he will remain unimpressive as long as he mistreats women. The kid was devastated. That was the point. From there, the two could discuss what it was he was doing, how it was viewed by those around him, and what he would need to do to correct this disappointing behavior.

English? Yes, he was a student in the man's English classes. This teacher cannot for the life of him remember his grade or how skilled he was at writing.

Doing the right things for the right reasons requires perspective, and developing that ability leads to accomplishments beyond academic prowess. Our purpose in education, moreover, is to prepare children for long-term success. A great deal of this preparation must be an insistence on the part of educators that students examine the world around them and be challenged to stretch their values, their opinions, and their understanding—to develop an impressive perspective.

Part Four

Conclusion

FOURTEEN

Autonomy

SETTING THE TONE

Setting a tone always works better than reacting to the aftermath of others' decisions. Great teachers have known this for as long as there have been classrooms full of children to educate. Impressive educators do not wait for students to drive them to drink before they react; rather, it is their planning that creates the safe and productive learning environment students deserve.

One administrator's first year as a dean of students was filled with extraordinary challenges. There were serious changes needed for the school (serious enough to create the dean of students position), and some of them were simply a matter of the adults in the building making a decision about something and following through with it.

Boys were accustomed to wearing hats, bandanas, and other accessories both unbecoming of academia and posing as potentials for gang colors and symbols. That needed to change. Some students did not agree with the decision to label certain items as contraband, but it happened nonetheless.

Cell phones were seen and heard throughout the school at all times. This, too, needed to change. Even more students disagreed with this decision, one that limited their ability and desire to text and talk around the clock, but it happened nonetheless.

The teachers were encouraged to be the adults in the building, not as monstrous ogres looking to hurt and hinder the student body, but rather as the mature experts who need not apologize for knowing what is best for the process of education.

This is what educational leaders (teachers and administrators) do in classrooms, in hallways, and at lunch tables when they know they are right about something—great teachers do the right things for the right reasons, and they sleep just fine at night.

So how does it happen that educators allow experts they have not met and generally do not trust to overrun what they are trying to accomplish in schools? Great public educators owe it to themselves and their public to protect students from the often harmful, generic, across-the-map public school ideologies created by these nameless, faceless experts.

Public school educators are still being led, subtly or not, by experts who either "just don't get it" or simply do not care enough to question their approaches. Why? For the same reason some school leaders allow students to text message their pals during an English test or wear gang attire that, by definition, intimidates or offends other students—because educators let them do it.

It could be said that K–12 public education has too many cooks in the kitchen. There are the students attending school, the local administrators and teachers delivering the product, the parents and other community members affected by the district, the occasionally present media to broadcast athletes and yearly test scores, and the incredibly important off-site state and government experts. Within this list of people, K–12 administrators typically spend their time serving local folks (students included) while trying to appease Big Brother. Serving two masters cannot work effectively.

In reality, there are simply too many people trying to tell the cooks what to make for supper. It has become incredibly easy for off-site experts to play an enormous role in the day-to-day proceedings of public schools. Unbelievably, curriculum realignment and subsequent class offerings can be turned upside down in schools because of unsightly test scores earned five hundred miles away in another district. Does anyone truly believe the curriculum-attainment problems of South Chicago are the problems of Lake Forest? Are the students of South St. Paul and the students of Fergus Falls similar enough to justify a shared curriculum?

Instead of reminding the community that they are the cooks and this is their kitchen, educational leaders in public schools have made it a habit of trying to make everyone happy. Further, they continue to bend over backward for state and federal educational landlords who habitually change the rules faster than educators can follow them.

The state- and federal-level ill informed will not disappear, of course, and those who do not know what educators know, regardless of their power, must be appropriately respected. That is, they are to be tolerated and their mandates that do not directly and specifically benefit students and communities should be followed to merely the smallest degree allowed by law.

Who is running the show with public schools if it is not local educators? If the study of education in this country has taught the public anything, it is that the less of an educational presence teachers and administrators (directly connected to students) have, the worse off the experience is for everyone. Do great teachers really want to shelve what they know works to focus instead on what takes seventeen in-service days to begin to comprehend?

Education is ripe for critiques and criticisms because everyone in this country, at least to some degree, has experience with it. However, if the ill informed are allowed to make decisions about educational issues, including what schools choose to emphasize, students will be hurt.

Being a high school student twenty years ago does not make one an expert in education. Caring about the education of a child, furthermore, does not make one an expert in education. Moreover, holding a state-level or higher position and taking great publicized pride in "fixing" education does not make one an expert in public education.

For teachers and administrators, perceiving and referring to one's self as an expert in education is not conceited banter, it is necessary. Further, it is what the public deserves. Honestly, what are teachers and administrators doing working as educators if they do not believe they know more than everyone else about this profession?

Most Americans could not fathom walking into a dentist's office and telling him or her how stupid the decision is to fill the cavity within a molar. Many would, perhaps, dislike the decision because of the inconvenience, the pain, and the expense, but most would opt to follow through with the twenty-first-century U.S. protocol of maintaining healthy teeth and gums.

Why? Because dentists do not apologize for being right. They went to school for a long time to become experts at teeth, and we did not. With this, it does not matter to our dentist that we have had teeth for the majority of our lives. She knows this, but she also knows that what we know about being a dentist and repairing teeth is the equivalent to what we know about being a surgeon after watching a few episodes of *Grey's Anatomy*.

Just as citizens need a dentist to be the expert he or she is, the public absolutely requires that public school teachers are educational experts. It often takes teachers over a decade in education, well over 10,000 hours, to realize this. It eventually dawns on great educators that most people do not understand enough about education—or the development of children—to make great decisions for everyone regarding these issues.

Further, public educators cannot be in the profession to impress everyone right here, right now. Public school teaching is the job of building students to become better and more successful people, even if that means periodically disappointing them.

Teachers also owe it to themselves to be the experts in education. There is no white-collar profession with a currently lower collective self-esteem than that of teachers. They have been society's punching bag for decades, and the instincts for fighting back have somehow been suppressed, probably because they have trained themselves to grin and bear it as it relates to top-down ideas about how to educate children.

FOLLOWING THROUGH

It takes courage to do the right things for the right reasons. Teachers and administrators work in, perhaps, the most challenging career in America. They are called to meet the needs of local children while simultaneously following the directives of distant authorities. Many educators (administrators included) have resigned themselves to simply do what they have been told. However, the best among teachers have proven it is possible to play the standard, assessment, and accountability game while also teaching young people how to be successful long after we finish testing them.

In the world of Core Standards and testing and AYP, what should public educators emphasize? Believe it or not, teachers actually can decide what they do *while* they are teaching students and *before* they take their tests. The remainder of this chapter provides a few examples of what the best K–12 educators are emphasizing in the face of inevitable public school realities.

TESTING OR TEACHING?

The tests are not going away. Students will be assessed, and public education's efforts will be scrutinized. Great educators are starting to view this situation as liberating because there is absolutely nothing to be done with the assessment train. School leaders can realize, however, that preparing students for tests is less effective than actually teaching them. They can realize, moreover, a few truths about test scores. First, teaching students a solid, well-rounded curriculum *is* preparing them for tests—and much more. Next, if the test scores remain insufficient after the delivery of a great curriculum, there was likely nothing that would have generated acceptable scores.

Good test scores? Please, the good test scores in this country were earned years before students filled in a single little oval with a number two pencil. Average to above-average intelligence? Did mom and dad read to you when you were young and maintain a strong presence as you aged? Yep, good test scores.

The choice is what to do with students when the state is not testing them. Secretaries and substitutes can give tests, not great teachers. Teachers work at educating all children, whether their moms and dads read to them years ago or not. Teachers also work at improving test scores—and *improving* test scores is far more indicative of good teaching than producing adequate test scores. The emphasis students deserve from their public schools is a daily commitment to educating them.

TRAINING OR EDUCATING?

Education is not training someone to do something. Capable students deserve the gift of thinking. Even within the simplest lessons taught in school, such as where students hang coats, how to sign out before using the restroom, or the difference between a notebook and a journal, children are better for knowing why they are asked to follow these guidelines and where else these methods could be implemented.

High-stakes testing runs the risk of training students to pass high-stakes tests. This by itself is not necessarily bad, but countless of these heavily trained students are transitioning from high school to college sorely lacking an ability to think critically. Along with proving they can isolate x in a mathematical equation and determine a theme within a short essay, students absolutely must be asked what does not fit into an oval: Why? How? What if?

FINISH LINE OR PROCESS?

Another negative side effect of approaching teaching as training is that students are often mistakenly perceived as finished products once they have been trained. After all, why keep teaching (and what would we teach?) once all the tests have been passed? The best keep teaching because the standards and associated tests are nothing more than milestones, and they may not even be that important.

Great coaches know that celebrating a Tuesday-night victory and viewing it as proof that their team has arrived is the easiest way possible to get embarrassed during Friday night's game. They know that shooting 92 percent from the free-throw line on Tuesday does not mean they can scratch free throws off the practice plan for Wednesday and Thursday.

They know this because they have seen their players react differently to different situations, they are aware of the highs and lows present with almost anything involving young people, and they care about their players enough to teach them to never, ever believe they have arrived at the finish line.

Great teachers are no different. The test scores are scoreboards and finish lines; other people can fret about these. The best teachers take students where they are and see to it that they incessantly practice and consistently improve.

The best college instructors view their classes as the Friday-night game. Almost all of their students won on Tuesday, and many of them have the GPA and ACT statistics to prove it. The opponent on Friday is a different team, however. These professors have found it remarkably easy to see which of their students have been taught to view education as a process and which have been allowed to believe that their accomplishments brought them to a finish line.

ADEQUATE OR MORE?

This is almost too obvious to write, but its importance for young people and their schools is such that it must be included: adequate yearly progress is not a victory for any students who are blessed enough to have average or higher capabilities and a safe, caring environment at home.

The job of great educators is not AYP accomplishment; the job is more, regardless of current status.

COMFORT FOR CUSTOMERS OR WORK AND ACCOMPLISHMENT?

The approach many administrators (especially within high schools) are taking to students' and their families' expectations of a day in school is questionable. As though high schools are competing with the local Holiday Inn for the best customer service reports, school leaders are making a habit of providing amazing creature comforts and liberties for students.

If school districts want to offer Subway and Dominoes in lunch lines, so be it. It behooves educators, however, to expect these well-fed students to remember they are eating lunch in a school. Subway employs people to make certain their sandwich wrappers and napkins are cleaned up after the patrons leave the restaurant, and students too often assume that service applies at school as well.

It has become common to see classroom furniture resembling basement lounge areas. High school classes decked out with a full-length sofa do provide a comforting presence for teenagers, and it is possible that these kids actually look forward to attending class because of these comforting additions. While observing one of her students practice-teach, one college professor recently sat in one of these comfortable classes. Four students crammed into the sofa, and one couple displayed more comfort than any of us should ever see in public.

To make matters worse, the cuddling couple were dressed for extraordinary comfort. The professor honestly cannot remember much about the lesson she was to observe that day. Instead, she recalls a sixteen-year-old girl dressed in pajama pants, a baggy T-shirt, and fluffy slippers intertwined with her sixteen-year-old boyfriend wearing baggy sweats and a world-class smile. One can only wonder how much of the lesson they remember.

We must also wonder what we are hoping to accomplish when high school upperclassmen are allowed, if not encouraged (we sell the possibility), to attend school part-time. These great kids have given their decade of school commitment, they passed their tests, and the least we can do is allow them some afternoon free time, so they are not asked to sit through a bunch of uninteresting classes they do not "need." Reality check: there is nothing these kids need more than to be annoyed in school.

But at least they are happy, right? Ridiculous. Public educators possess the autonomy to slow down the trend of ensuring short-term happiness to instead focus energy on preparing students for long-term success. Great teachers have a job to do, and it is being marginalized by the conflicting expectations of customer service.

APOLOGIZING OR LEADING?

Behind closed doors, K–12 school leaders lament focusing on top-down educational initiatives. This is because public school success stories have absolutely nothing to do with reproducible minutiae. Schools succeed because of one or more no-nonsense, tough-as-nails, positive, and inspirational educational leaders.

The program or initiative they develop? It was created based on what their students and their community needed at that time. Provided these leaders accurately determined what was needed, almost any method of delivery and catchy title would have sufficed.

And what do students and their respective community members oftentimes need? They need a kick in the pants. Immense school and district turnaround does not materialize from educators suddenly deciding to teach English and math; it happens when educators (or at least a few great educational leaders) decide they are going to do whatever it takes to make their students and community members care about English and math.

Ironically, large-scale school-district overhauls, especially within urban areas, are the result of desperation. These districts suffer under the assessment-and-accountability umbrella and are either resigned to failing miserably or abandon the standards-and-testing emphasis as much as possible.

The miracle stories that surface periodically are the result of desperate, strong educators changing a school culture. Students begin to experience success shortly after they experience caring and commitment in the form of expectations and accountability. Change for the better happens when students show up on time every day, when they work harder than they have ever been asked to work, and when respect and decency become habitual.

The tests are unavoidable. Likewise, some of our most inspirational leaders have learned that without emphasizing the right habits, poor test scores are also unavoidable.

Index

abilities, student, vii
academics: as parental priority, 4, 15; responsibility in, 100; sports compared to, 89; teaching to test and measurable, 54
academic standards: in curriculum, 33; merely adequate, 79–80; parents and teachers creating, 35–36; policy concerning, 20; politics concerning, 19; responsibility in, 100–101; social need for, 33; for teachers, 41–42; work ethic and, 79–80. *See also* assessment and testing; state standards
accountability: politics over, 20; public education and focus on, ix, viii; school leaders' balancing assessment and, ix
adequate yearly progress (AYP): in assessment, ix, 20; for best students, 55–56; inadequacy of, 118
administrators: families and students wooed by, 15–18; student recognition for, 90–92; on teachers' lesson plans, 37; tone set by, 113–114, 114–116. *See also* educational leaders
adults: in assessment and testing, 35; on assessment and testing, 53; caring and student failure, 46–47; in character education, 44–46; in communication skills, 61; education as priority for, 5; gratification delayed from, 95, 96–97; narcissism from, 88, 89; perspective from, 105, 105–106; politics shortsighting, 19; respect, decency, and humility from, 92–93; responsibility assumed by, 97–98; responsibility taught by, 98–99, 99–100, 101; student engagement and discipline from, 7–9, 32–33, 34; students and impact of, xii, 5, 45, 49; in teaching respect, decency, and humility, 87–88. *See also* family and families; parents
air travel, 97
apology and apologists, 119
appeasement: caring and, 46; educational leaders and social, 15–18; of students, 63
assessment and testing: adults in, 35; adults on, 53; AYP in, ix, 20; character education impact on, 44; curriculum and, xi; deficiencies in, ix–x; limited writing ability and, x; perspective in, 105; politics over, 20; public education and focus on, ix, viii, x, 55; school leaders' balancing accountability and, ix; social need for, 33; state standards and, 35, 39; student achievement impacted by, ix, 107–108; student engagement compared to, 32; student success and parameters for, xiv, 56; by teachers, 38; teachers on, 41–42; teaching compared to, 116; teaching impact of, xi, xii, xii–xiii. *See also* academic standards; teaching to test
Atchison, Andrew, 36; character education for, 44–45; family of, 32–33, 35–36; graduation standards' impact on, 30; *Macbeth* and life experience of, 30–31; student engagement of, 30–31, 32; student performance of, 30; on teachers, 33
attendance. *See* time, timeliness, and attendance
autonomy: apology compared to leadership in, 119; of educators, xiv, 116–119; finish line or process

121

emphasized in, 117–118; setting tone in, 113–116; in student comfort *versus* work ethic, 118–119; teachers engendering, 113; testing or teaching in, 116; training or educating in, 117

AYP. *See* adequate yearly progress

behavior, as learned, 87

bigger picture, in perspective, 104

caring: appeasement and, 46; about curriculum and extracurricular activities, 47; about sports, 47; student achievement and, 46; about student desires, 46–47, 47; student failure and adult, 46–47; about student needs, 47

character education: adults in, 44–46; assessment impact of, 44; of Atchison, 44–45; in educational reform, 43–44; for lower class students, 43–44; for middle and upper class students, 44; in public education, 45; social impact of, 45; in unwritten curriculum, 43; U.S. impact from, 45

classroom and classroom success: critical thinking taught in, 57; curriculum attainment and, 9; timeliness and attendance in, 72

college and college readiness: communication skills in, 62–63, 107; critical thinking in, 57, 107; deficiencies in, ix–x, vii; grandparents on contemporary, 69; public education and, 39, 42, 49; from teaching to test, 53

comfort: in communication skills, 61, 63–64; student work ethic *versus*, 118–119. *See also* dress

communication skills, age-appropriate: from adults, 61; in college readiness, 62–63, 107; comfort and convenience in, 61, 63–64; through dress, 62–64; education in, 66; human interaction in, 65–67; parents' intervention impacting, 66; teachers engendering, 66–67;

technology literacy and, 64–65; in unwritten curriculum, 48. *See also* human interaction

convenience, 61, 63–64

conversation skills, 65–66

Core Standards: changes to, 35; state, 35

courage, 56

critical thinking: classroom and teaching, 57; in college readiness, 57, 107; courage from, 56; without rubric, 57–58; teachers engendering, 54, 58; teaching, 56–59; teaching to test compared to, 54, 55

curriculum: academic standards in, 33; assessment and, xi; classroom success and attainment of, 9; coordinator, 29; extracurricular activities balanced against, 47; public education and focus on, ix, viii; student engagement compared to, 32; student success through attainment of, 77–78; for teachers, 41–42. *See also* unwritten curriculum

decency. *See* respect, decency, and humility

decisions: in education from teachers, 116; human interaction and defending, 65; student success defined by, 99–100

dedication. *See* work ethic and dedication

deficiencies: in assessment and testing, ix–x; in college readiness, ix–x, vii; of national policies, 21; in public education, vii–viii; in student habits, xi, xi–xii; in student motivation, vii, viii, xi, xi–xii

Democrats: in funding, 22–23; public education impact of, 23, 23–24

desires, student, 46–47, 47

dress: communication skills through, 62–64; student habits regarding, 61–64

Duckworth, Angela Lee, 77

education: as adult priority, 5; in communication skills, 66;

educational leaders and policy example for, 15–18; educators' power in, 14, 114–116; as parental priority, 4, 15; politics and social demands concerning, 24; public, parental, and student role in, 15, 20; of society, 14; student performance in, viii; of teachers, 41; teachers deciding emphasis of, 116; test scores as symptom of, 39–40; training compared to, 117. *See also* character education; public education

educational leaders: education policy example for, 16–18; ill-informed or ill-willed and response of, 14; social appeasement from, 15–18; student learning for, 15, 72; teachers identified by, 9; on teaching to test, 53; in tone setting, 113–114

educational reform: character education in, 43–44; technology in, 64

educators: autonomy of, xiv, 116–119; dysfunctional families, social responsibility, and, 11–14; education and power of, 14, 114–116; families and role of, 24–25; new policy and, 20; public conflicting with, 3–4; student discipline and tough love from, 7–9; student habits emphasized by, xiv; in student learning, viii; in student success, 6–7

entitlement: of gifted students, 70, 71; from parents, 70–71; student discipline and, 7, 45, 70–71. *See also* gratification

extracurricular activities: responsibility and teamwork in, 100; traditional curriculum balanced against, 47

eye contact, 65

facts, in student success, 53–54, 54
failure: adult caring and student, 46–47; dedication through, 81; example of, 81–82; necessity of, 82; perspective in, 103–105; in public schools, 81; teaching how to handle, 81–83; writing, 82–83

family and families: administrators wooing, 15–18; of Atchison, 32–33, 35–36; educators and dysfunctional, 11–14; educators role and, 24–25; respect, decency, and humility in, 87. *See also* parents

finish line, 117–118

Friday Night Tykes, 106

funding: Democrats and Republicans in, 22–23; politics over, 19, 20–21, 22; in public education, 22; wasteful, 20–21

grades: defining, 107; as necessary, 108; perspective on, 107–108

graduation standards: Atchison and impact of, 30; state, 29, 30, 34–36, 39

grandparents: contemporary college for, 69; gratification delayed by, 95–96; parents and public education for, 6; on timeliness and attendance, 69

gratification: adults and delaying, 95, 96–97; grandparents delaying, 95–96; responsibility, teamwork, and delaying, 95–97

greatness, 74–75

higher education, ix

homework: perspective regarding, 108; public schools' eliminating, 74

human interaction: in communication skills, 65–67; conversation skills, 65–66; defending decisions in, 65; eye contact in, 65

humility. *See* respect, decency, and humility

ill-informed or ill-willed: educational leaders response to, 14; in society, 11–14

leadership. *See* educational leaders; school leaders and leadership

learning: behavior, 87; difficulty of, 55; education leaders and student, 15, 72; Profile of, 29, 34; students as always, 71–72; work ethic and

dedication in, 78. *See also* student learning
lesson plans: administrators on teachers', 37; ineffective, 38; substitute teachers and, 37, 37–38
luck, 88

Macbeth (Shakespeare), 30–31
Minnesota: graduation standards in, 29, 30, 34–36, 39; Profile of Learning, 29, 34
mission statements: example of, 80; of school districts, 80–83; work ethic and dedication in, 80–83

narcissism: from adults, 88, 89; respect, decency, humility, and, 88–89; from sports, 88–89; talent and, 90
NEA Today, 21, 22, 23

outcome-based education (OBE), 20

parents: academics or education as priority for, 4, 15; academic standards from, 35–36; in character education, 45; communication skills and intervention of, 66; educational leaders' appeasement of, 15; education and role of, 15, 20; entitlement from, 70–71; gifted students and, 90; grandparents on public education and, 6; public schools and, 4; responsibility and teamwork taught by, 99; role of, xiv, 4, 7, 12; student discipline and tough love from, 7–8; student habits and, 4–5; in student success, 6, 33; time management from, 74; work ethic from, 79, 81
perspective: from adults, 105, 105–106; in assessment and testing, 105; bigger picture in, 104; in failure, 103–105; on grades and test scores, 107–108; regarding homework, 108; in sports, 103–105, 106–107; on student success, 109–110; teaching students, xiii, 105–106, 109–110; in unwritten curriculum, 49
Plato, 19

policy and policy makers: for academic standards, 20; deficiencies of national, 21; educators and new, 20; politics and, 21; on public education deficiencies, viii; tone setting and, 113–114
politics, politicians, and political rhetoric: adults' shortsighted from, 19; education and social demands on, 24; over assessment and accountability, 20; over funding, 19, 20–21, 22; Plato on, 19; policy and, 21; public education as social responsibility and, 20; public education trivialized by, 19–20, 23–25; for teachers, 21–25; in teaching, 19
POPS. *See* Pride of Pirates
Postman, Neil, 43
Pride of Pirates (POPS), 91–93
private schools, 17–18
process, 117–118
profession, teaching as, 15–16
Profile of Learning, 29, 34
public and public opinion: education and role of, 15, 20; educators conflict with, 3–4; of public education, 3–4
public education: accountability and curriculum focus in, ix, viii; assessment focus in, ix, viii, x, 55; character education in, 45; college readiness and, 39, 42, 49; deficiencies in, vii–viii; Democrats' impact on, 23, 23–24; dysfunctional families, social responsibility, and, 11–14; funding in, 22; grandparents on parents and, 6; politics trivializing, 19–20, 23–25; public opinion of, 3–4; Republicans impact on, 23–24; social or cultural responsibility in, 14, 20; teaching to test and ideology of, 54; in U.S., vii, xii, 3
public schools: administrators wooing students in, 15–18; failure in, 81; homework elimination in, 74; parents and, 4; respect, decency, and humility in, 87; safety in, 90–91; sports' role in, 4, 7; students in, 55;

teachers in, 3–4

reflection, 38
Republicans: in funding, 22, 22–23; public education impact of, 23–24
respect, decency, and humility, xiii, 48–49; from adults, 92–93; adults in, 87–88; all worthy of, 86–87; example of showing, 85–87; narcissism and, 88–89; in public schools, 87; public school safety and, 90–91; student recognition for, 90–92; teaching, 87–88
response-to-intervention (RTI), 20
responsibility and teamwork, 49; in academics, 100; academic standards and, 100–101; adults assuming, 97–98; adults teaching, 98–99, 99–100, 101; in air travel, 97; decisions defining success in, 99–100; examples of, 101–102; in extracurricular activities, 100; gratification delayed in, 95–97; redefining, 97–99; to self and society, xiii; from teachers, 100, 101; teaching, 98–99, 99–102. *See also* social or cultural responsibility
RTI. *See* response-to-intervention
rubric, 57–58

safety, public school, 90–91
school and school day: for teaching responsibility and teamwork, 100–102; for teaching timeliness and attendance, 72–74. *See also* public schools
school districts, mission statement for, 80–83
school leaders and leadership: assessment and accountability balanced for, ix; autonomy and apology compared for, 119. *See also* educational leaders
Shakespeare, William, 30–31
social or cultural responsibility: dysfunctional families, educators, and, 11–14; example of, 11–14; in public education, 14, 20

society: academic standards and assessment needed in, 33; character education impact on, 45; educational leaders and appeasement of, 15–18; education of, 14; ill-informed and ill-willed in, 11–14; politics and education demands of, 24; responsibility to, xiii
soft skills, 77–78
sports: academics compared to, 89; caring about, 47; narcissism from, 88–89; perspective in, 103–105, 106–107; public schools and role of, 4, 7; youth, 106
state standards: Core, 35; curriculum coordinator and, 29; for graduation, 29, 30, 34–36, 39; testing and, 35, 39
student achievement and success: assessment and testing impact on, ix, 107–108; assessment parameters for, xiv, 56; caring and, 46; curriculum attainment for, 77–78; decision defining, 99–100; educators in, 6–7; from effective teaching, 39; facts in, 53–54, 54; parents in, 6, 33; perspective regarding, 109–110; qualities to emphasize in, xii; student discipline as, 9; U.S., vii; work ethic and, 77–78, 78
student engagement, motivation, and discipline: adults in, 7–9, 32–33, 34; assessment and curriculum compared to, 32; deficiencies in, vii, viii, xi, xi–xii; entitlement and, 7, 45, 70–71; recognition of, 30–32; as student success, 9; teachers in, 8–9, 34, 40; teaching, 9
student habits: deficiencies in, xi, xi–xii; regarding dress, 61–64; educator emphasis on, xiv; parents and, 4–5; in unwritten curriculum, 48–49. *See also* communication skills, age-appropriate; critical thinking; responsibility and teamwork; thinking skills, age-appropriate; time, timeliness, and attendance; work ethic and dedication

student learning: for educational leaders, 15, 72; educators in, viii; long-term, xiii

student needs: caring about, 47; in unwritten curriculum, 48

student performance: of Atchison, 30; in education, viii; in higher education, ix

student recognition: for administrators, 90–92; of majority of students, 90; for respect, decency, and humility, 90–92

students: abilities of, vii, xii; administrators, parents, teachers, and gifted, 90; administrators wooing, 15–18; adult caring and failure of, 46–47; adults' impact on, xii, 5, 45, 49; as always learning, 71–72; appeasement of, 63; AYP for best, 55–56; character education for lower class, 43–44; character education for middle and upper class, 44; comfort *versus* work ethic for, 118–119; desires of, 46–47, 47; education and role of, 15; entitlement of gifted, 70, 71; in public schools, 55; student recognition of majority of, 90; teaching perspective to, xiii, 105–106, 109–110; technology and impact on, 43; time management by, 73–74

substitute teachers, 37, 37–38

talent: as luck, 88; narcissism and, 90

teachers: academic standards, assessment, and curriculum for, 41–42; academic standards from, 35–36; administrators on lesson plans of, 37; assessment by, 38; Atchison on, 33; beginning, 41; communication skills engendered by, 66–67; critical thinking engendered by, 54, 58; educating or training by, 117; educational leaders identifying, 9; education emphasis lying with, 116; education of, 41; evolution of, 41–42; gifted students for, 90; great, 39–40; Minnesota standards and, 29; in perspective and student success, 109–110; politics for, 21–25; in public schools, 3–4; reflection by, 38; responsibility and teamwork from, 100, 101; role of, xii–xiii, 7–9, 38–40; in student engagement and discipline, 8–9, 34, 40; substitute, 37, 37–38; teaching objectives of, 38; teaching or testing by, 116; timeliness and attendance for, 72–74; tone set by, 113–114, 114–116. *See also* autonomy; educators; lesson plans

teacher traits and habits: self-focus on, 41; teacher education on, 41

teaching: assessment impact on, xi, xii, xii–xiii; critical thinking, 56–59; finish line compared to process in, 117–118; how to handle failure, 81–83; perspective to students, xiii, 105–106, 109–110; political rhetoric in, 19; as profession, 15–16; respect, decency, and humility, 87–88; responsibility and teamwork, 98–99, 99–102; student achievement from effective, 39; student discipline, 9; teachers' objectives in, 38; testing compared to, 116; timeliness and attendance during school day, 72–74; work ethic and dedication, 78, 81

teaching to test: academic measurement in, 54; adults on, 53; college readiness from, 53; critical thinking compared to, 54, 55; educational leaders on, 53; public education ideology and, 54; student success, facts, and, 54; thinking skills and, 53–55

teamwork. *See* responsibility and teamwork

technology and technology literacy: communication skills and, 64–65; ease of use, 64–65; in educational reform, 64; students and impact of, 43

10,000 hour rule, 75

testing. *See* assessment and testing

test scores: as education symptom, 39–40; as necessary, 108; perspective on, 107–108
thinking skills, age-appropriate: teaching to test and, 53–55; in unwritten curriculum, 48. *See also* critical thinking
time, timeliness, and attendance, 48; in classroom, 72; grandparents on, 69; greatness from putting in, 74–75; guidelines for teaching, 72–74; necessity of, 72–73; parents on management of, 74; students as always learning in, 71–72; students' management of, 73–74; 10,000 hour rule in, 75; value of everyday, 73
tone, setting: administrators and teachers in, 113–114, 114–116; in autonomy, 113–116; educational leaders and policy makers in, 113–114
tough love, 7–9
training, educating compared to, 117

United States (U.S.): character education and impact in, 45; ill-informed or ill-willed in, 11–14; public education in, vii, xii, 3; student success in, vii
unwritten curriculum, xiii; character education in, 43; communication skills in, 48; on student habits, 48–49; student needs in, 48
U.S. *See* United States

work ethic and dedication, 48; academic standards and, 79–80; attention lacking for, 77; through failure, 81; in learning, 78; from parents, 79, 81; in school district mission statements, 80–83; as soft skills, 77–78; student achievement and, 77–78, 78; teaching, 78, 81
writing and writing ability: assessment and limited, x; failure involving, 82–83

About the Author

John Elling Tufte is a professor of education. He has taught and coached at the high school level, worked as a secondary administrator, and now presents to and consults with teachers, administrators, and parents about issues facing schools today.

www.ingramcontent.com/pod-product-compliance
Lightning Source LLC
Chambersburg PA
CBHW021846220426
43663CB00005B/421